Prison Break

Vanquish the Victim, Own Your Obstacles,
and Lead Your Life

Jason Goldberg

Published by Best Seller Publishing®, Pasadena, CA
Best Seller Publishing® is a registered trademark
Printed in the United States of America.
ISBN-13: 978-1537705811
ISBN-10: 1537705814

This publication is designed to provide accurate and authoritative information with regard to the subject matter covered. It is sold with the understanding that the publisher is not engaged in rendering legal, accounting, or other professional advice. If legal advice or other expert assistance is required, the services of a competent professional should be sought. The opinions expressed by the authors in this book are not endorsed by Best Seller Publishing® and are the sole responsibility of the author rendering the opinion.

Most Best Seller Publishing® titles are available at special quantity discounts for bulk purchases for sales promotions, premiums, fundraising, and educational use. Special versions or book excerpts can also be created to fit specific needs.

For more information, please write:
Best Seller Publishing®
1346 Walnut Street, #205
Pasadena, CA 91106
or call 1(626) 765 9750
Toll Free: 1(844) 850-3500

Visit us online at: www.BestSellerPublishing.org

To Steve Chandler for coming up with the title for this book.

…and for being my partner in *Not-So-Serious* crime

…and for being an incredible mentor

…and for inspiring me to write books

…and for giving me the permission to be funny in my work (*'permission' is, of course, not the same as 'ability'*)

…and for showing me what an original I truly am

…and for being a friend

…oh, and for being so sincerely devoted to and invested in my growth and success and fundamentally shifting the entire way I see the world, without which none of the work I do, the impact I make, or the fun I am having in life would have been nearly as sustainable or fulfilling.

So yeah, thanks for all of that.

> *"God writes a lot of comedy...the trouble is,*
> *he's stuck with so many bad actors*
> *who don't know how to play funny."*

— Garrison Keillor

Table of Contents

Acknowledgements

Wow, a book! A real book! Stories, thoughts, ideas (hopefully some with some actual value) extracted from my head and etched (metaphorically) onto the page. How in the heck did I ever get here? Oh yeah, I remember...

To Amir Karkouti, for always being exactly the kind of friend I needed, for treating me like a brother, encouraging the crap out of me, and inspiring me by how you show up as an entrepreneur, a coach, a writer, and a human being. I love you, man!

To Christina Berkley, my SSCB, for always loving on and celebrating me so genuinely, for your random video love notes, and for what an absolutely fearless, powerful badass you are in the world.

To Jacob Sokol, personal growth may have brought us together, but it is F-bombs, brotherhood, and East Coast hip-hop that will keep us connected. Thank you for being the conduit into so much of the world I am immersed in today and for being an ever-present example of creativity, service, and soul-centered awesomeness.

To Sean Stephenson, thank you for mentoring me to become an exponentially better speaker and more importantly, for challenging me in the way that only you can, teaching me to really look within and see my opportunities for true expansion. I love and honor you, brother.

To Brian Johnson, for Entheos, for your story, for your gift of wisdom-sharing, for the opportunity to teach at the Academy for Optimal Living, and for creating Philosophers Notes which, when given to me as a gift in 2011, opened up all new possibilities for what my life and business could become.

To Byron Katie, for the gift of "The Work" and for the understanding you have taught me to experience truth and freedom. I am forever grateful to you for sharing your wisdom in a way that resonates so deeply with me and for your wicked sense of humor that captivates and inspires me whether I am physically in a room with you or simply reading your books.

To my momma, Linda, for all of your sacrifice, hard work, and patience in raising me as a single mother. I know it couldn't have been easy—especially in those early teen years—yikes! And I am truly grateful for how you always loved and provided for me no matter what. You are a hustler for sure! You raised me with so much love and support, and it is the reason it is so natural for me to love and give so much of myself to others now.

To my uncle Philip Golabuk, my UPD, thank you for being such a powerful and present father figure to me as I was growing up (I'll never forget our Saturdays together), for literally "driving me up the wall," and for setting an example of the importance of not living an "unexamined life." I am so thankful to have you in my world!

I can hear my editor playing the Academy Awards wrap up music, so I'd also like to thank other super supportive, inspirational and wonderful people in my life (in no particular order): My bros at Storyboard Media (Ben, Justin and Hemed), Devon Bandison ("my man!"), Natalie Alexia, Cecilia Sardeo, Kyle Cease, Chris Dorris (a.k.a. "TV"), Mia Lux Koning, Julia Rose, Ajit Nawalkha, Mandy Lehto, Dr. Pete McAlindon, Phil Goddard, David Gerber, Eric Luczak, Steve Hardison, Vishen Lakhiani, Nick Huntington, Pat Divilly, Maru Iabichela, Isabelle Tierney, Allen Kupetz, Troy McGuire, Chrysztyna Rowek, Hannah Zambrano, Kshitij Minglani, Mark J. Silverman, Irene Giovanna Ricotta, Meredith Bell, Kathy Chandler, Danny McElhinny, Dr. Susan Bach, Angela Balestreri and Scott Taylor.

To my private clients, the participants in my group coaching programs, our loyal "The Not-So-Serious Life Show" viewers, and the attendees of my talks and trainings, thank you for your incredible feedback, your engagement, your love and trust and for living what you learned so it didn't turn from self-help into "shelf-help." I am eternally grateful to each and every one of you!

And to anyone I may have forgotten to thank here, whether for a reason, a season or for a lifetime, you showed up in my world, and I am a better, stronger human being because of you! Thank you!

Now, onto the show!

The Day the Universe Cut Me Off

> *Men occasionally stumble over the truth, but most of them pick themselves up and hurry off as if nothing ever happened.*
>
> —Winston S. Churchill

So there I am, mouth full of donut, head full of confusion, and body full of rage all because of Amazon.com and my stupid bank?

I want to take you back to 2009. I don't know the date. I think it was summer, but in Florida where I was living at the time; you can never tell because there are only two seasons, "hot" and "hot as hell." But I know it was a Wednesday.

I know it was a Wednesday because it was staff meeting day at the tech firm where I was the director of operations and engineering…

which also meant it was donut day. Which means it was also the day I would do the dance where I would eat just half a donut during the meeting to show my control and restraint, and then after the meeting was over, I would sneak back in and eat at least two more donuts. The entire time, I would be looking around corners and worrying that my co-workers or boss would catch me and reveal my shameful secret.

So I took my double fisting of donuts back to my big beautiful corner office with a wall of windows overlooking downtown Orlando (the home of Mickey Mouse and the old Jewish members of my family who could no longer stand New York winters). I sat back in my comfy leather chair, pulled up to my huge high-definition monitor, and did what anyone in upper management does when they have a day full of challenging projects and fires to put out—I started browsing the Internet.

I eventually made it over to Amazon.com where I searched for some fun socks because I am just a little bit obsessed with fun and stylish dress socks—it's just about all we have as men to show our individuality!

After a marathon clicking session, I finally found a pair of awesome argyle socks—okay, six pairs of awesome argyle socks. I added them to my shopping cart, fist pumped because they were Amazon Prime eligible and would be here in two days, and popped in my credit card number.

I pressed the "confirm order" button, but as I started to stand and shove the last quarter chunk of donut number two into my mouth, I was shocked, because I saw a message pop up on my computer monitor that was as foreign to me, at the time, as a plate of vegetables: "Card Declined."

I sat back down a bit confused and a bit more angry; verified I had typed the card number, expiration date, and the super secret three-digit code correctly; and pressed submit. Again, I was taunted by this message telling me that my order could not be completed because my card was declined. The automated message said I would need to contact my bank for further assistance.

"What the hell is going on?" I thought. I was only in my late 20s at the time, but I was making over $100,000 per year at my job and knew that my $70 order of socks wasn't going to break the bank. So I reacted at that moment like I did anytime something didn't go exactly according to plan. I exploded!

I immediately felt a rush of blood, heat, and rage run through my veins. This was just how I operated at this time in my life. Everything was a big deal. I could spill a glass of water or have my house burn down, and I would react the same way because I had so little control over myself. I was a *Prisoner* of the world around me.

So I was getting more and more upset and thinking about how I was a busy man, especially now that I had wasted 30 minutes surfing for socks. Pissed off that my card was being declined, I threw my chair back into the wall behind me, snatched up my cell phone from my desk, flung open my office door, and stomped out into the lobby of my office building to scream at my bank for this ridiculous inconvenience.

After getting frustrated with the voice recognition on the customer service line and smashing the zero button ten times to get a live person, I finally heard a human on the other side of the phone. "Thank you for calling the banking support line. This is Steven. How can I help you?"

My better judgment stopped me from an all out, R-rated verbal assault, but I did lay into Steven as if he were personally responsible for my card getting declined. I insisted he tell me this instant why my new socks were not on their way to a mail sorting facility right now.

Of course, Steven was kind and eerily calm when he replied (because that's what Steven was trained to do) and said, "Mr. Goldberg, I truly apologize for the inconvenience. It seems our system flagged potentially fraudulent activity on your account, so your card has been deactivated pending a review of the charges. This is for your protection."

My first thought was, "*You* are the one who is going to need protection." My second thought was, "What?? Fraudulent activity? Like someone stole my identity? Hacked my bank account?"

Now, at the height of my frustration and anger, I demanded to know what these fraudulent charges were that had hijacked my day, my money, and my emotions! What Steven would say to me after some feverish typing on his keyboard would rock my world at its core.

See, one thing you need to know about me is that from a very young age, I was known as someone with a great personality. If you have never had someone use "great personality" as the only superlative to describe you, let me fill you in on a little secret. For me at least, this was code for "Jason is a nice guy but fat and unfortunately unattractive."

Being morbidly obese was a feeling I had always been familiar with. I had been a "big kid" my entire life. At the age of 15, I tipped the scales at 250 pounds. You remember being 15, right? The time in our lives when kids are considerate, loving, and accepting of who we are on the inside and completely disregard our appearance. Yeah, exactly!

So on this particular Wednesday in 2009, though it was a snapshot of, up to that point, the most successful time of my life professionally, it was the most challenging time in my life personally, because I was struggling, barely living at a weight of 332 pounds! Thirty-five percent of my body was fat. I was dying a slow death and feeling so depressed, angry, hopeless and even, at times, suicidal that sometimes the slow death seemed a little too slow for my liking.

I had plenty of excuses as to why and how this happened.

I was raised by a single mother who worked lots of hours, so fast food and pizza were staple foods in our household.

I lived in Florida where it was hot 11 months out of the year, so I couldn't go outside and play or exercise—I was *forced* to stay inside and watch television or play video games.

As I got older, I would say things like "Oh, but I worked hard today at school (or work), so I deserve to 'veg out' and go numb in front of the TV (or the computer)."

Oh and then, of course, there is genetics—one of those fascinating subjects that we can be completely ignorant about and still blame with all of the confidence in the world for our bodies, our health, and our shortcomings.

The common denominator and my core belief were that it was never under my control, and I was always a Prisoner to circumstances—to the weight of the world that I believed was responsible for putting the weight on my body.

So I asked Steven, still holding on to a mix of anger and curiosity, "Tell me, what were the fraudulent charges? What did these morons buy with *my* money?" I was expecting to hear about extravagant

rooms at the Waldorf, bottles of champagne at a swanky New York nightclub, or a limited edition signed Lady Gaga meat suit.

But instead Steven said, "Mr. Goldberg, it seems that there were transactions at four fast restaurants...that all occurred yesterday... all in the Orlando area. So our system assumed someone had stolen your credit card and were testing it by making small purchases at various establishments."

The line went silent. I thought to myself that this had to be some kind of cruel joke. I mean, I *had* eaten all of that fast food in one day, but was that such a big deal? Did a multi-billion dollar bank just tell me that my eating habits were out of control—that I could no longer be trusted to have easy access to financial means to feed my habit and that it was their job to cut me off?

"Mr. Goldberg, are you there? Did I lose you?"

I was there, but I absolutely felt lost. Because as much as I searched in that moment to find a person, a situation, something outside of me to blame for this rampage of unhealthy choices—I couldn't.

And that was when it hit me. What had me struggling in my body, in my mind, and in my life wasn't that I needed better genetics. It wasn't that I needed more home-cooked meals or more comfortable weather.

It was quite simply personal responsibility, *Self-Leadership* that was missing in my world. I finally admitted to myself that if there is a problem, then I am the problem. This was beautiful, freeing, and powerful (eventually—it certainly didn't feel that way in the moment) because if I am the problem, then I am also the solution!

Over the course of the next two years, I took full ownership of my health and was able to lose over 130 pounds.

While I'd love to tell you that everything changed for the better when I lost the weight, the truth is, it didn't, because I wasn't only overweight in my body. The financial juggernaut that cut me off from continuing my fast food world tour was also bringing to light all of the other types of weight I had been holding on to my entire life.

I know we typically measure weight in pounds, stones, or kilos. But it can also be measured in dollars (my anxiety over money), milligrams (the high dose of anti-depressants I was on), thoughts, limitations, and beliefs (that I would never be good enough, lovable, successful, attractive; that I would never get the permission I thought I needed to take risks, fall in love with uncertainty, and truly be myself, unapologetically).

You may be asking yourself, "Why does any of this even matter? Isn't all of this other weight you're talking about—the anger, the sadness, the depression—just feelings? Are you trying to tell me that I can't just fake my way through or ignore this 'weight' and grind, hustle, and work my way to success? Aren't you just some new age hipster who wants us to get in touch with our inner children?"

Listen, whatever you do on your time is your business. But no, they aren't just "feelings." If that were true, they might be manageable. How many people do we know who try to "manage" them with food, drugs, alcohol, sex, or any other number of coping mechanisms?

It is much more impactful and pervasive in our experience of the world than you think. Because when we would otherwise be enthusiastic, creative, peaceful, producing real value in the world, and doing things that set our souls on fire, all of this weight has a huge added side effect. This weight was the cause of me waiting to be and do all of the things I desired to be and do in the world.

Waiting to leave my corporate job because I had tied my self-worth to my net worth and without my title and salary, I feared being identity- and purposeless.

Waiting to have weight loss surgery because people might think of me as lazy, taking the easy way out, or weak.

Waiting to show my humorous and playful side and use it as the gift that it is for fear that no one would take me "seriously."

Waiting to have the perfect website and customer avatar before I could start my speaking and coaching business because otherwise, it would be a failure and I would have to go back to a miserable corporate job.

Waiting for approval from mentors and more courageous trailblazers instead of just choosing to experiment and tweak my path as needed.

Waiting to pull the plug on my first startup because I didn't want the investors and mentors who had put their trust in me to hate me.

Waiting to ask for a sale from clients because I didn't want to be pushy or salesy even though I knew I had already truly served them and helped them change their lives.

Waiting to write this book because of fear that it wouldn't be life-changing enough or live up to some expectation of what it should look like.

So not only was I overweight, I was also "over wait"!

The funny thing is that time did nothing to help these situations. In fact, the longer I waited, the more weight I gained in all aspects and the heavier my life felt.

Where are you holding on to weight? What are you waiting to be, do, or create in your world? Where are you waiting to break free from being a Prisoner so that you can step into the *Self-Leader* that has always been inside of you?

If I checked your universal bank account and reviewed the transaction log of your life, where would I see you were overspending, carrying debt, procrastinating, investing in things (or people or beliefs or stories) that don't serve you, and making choices that are holding you back from experiencing prosperity or being your best self? Where are the opportunities for a prison break to occur in your life?

Remember what I said earlier, that if there is a problem, then I am the problem. And if I am the problem, I am also the solution.

Once you are ready and willing to test this, know that there is a solution, a simple truth, an undeniable distinction that is rooted in something you already possess within you right now. It all starts with a decision you can make today.

It is the choice to be aware when you are seeing the world as a Prisoner of circumstance; to no longer be held captive by your inner dialog, your past, or the limitations you have created in your own mind (or been gifted by well-meaning people from your past); and to instead embrace true Self-Leadership.

It is a way of being that is not about the power of positive thinking, or rainbows and butterflies, or living in a delusional view of the world. Instead, it's about possibility-based thinking. It is about operating from the power of a clear, calm, purposeful mind that seeks the truth instead of succumbing to a story. A mind that then knows exactly what actions to take to create an incredibly happy, peaceful and prosperous life and business.

In short, when faced with the inevitable challenges, confusion, uncertainty, and strife that life sometimes presents to us, it is asking yourself "If there were a way to use this for my greatest good, what would it be?" or "What is trying to emerge from within me that will fundamentally change the way I see the world?"

A few people close to me urged me not to use the term *Prisoner* to describe the way I approached life for the first 30 years of it because I have never been physically incarcerated.

But then I watched a TEDx Talk delivered inside of a real prison by one of my good friends, Dr. Sean Stephenson. He talked about meeting people every day who aren't surrounded by guards and electrical fences but who are no freer than the people who were forced to be within the walls of the facility in which he was speaking.

I realized then that even though I had never been put into a cell and forced to live my life on other people's terms and schedules, I had been imprisoned by my mind with my own inner warden, correctional officers, and even a baby assassin (more on that later) for almost my entire life.

Luckily, I also realized that the ways I had reacted and how I had lived in the past were nothing more than a date on the calendar. My past choices, beliefs, and missteps are not some permanent, pervasive part of my DNA. Whether 10 years ago, 10 weeks ago or 10 minutes ago, they have no bearing on what I will create and who I can become in this very moment. And since the past and the future are just concepts, memories, and fabrications that don't exist in reality, "this very moment" is the only one we actually have.

Before diving into the rest of this book, I also want to share a few notes about how I wrote it and how you can use it most effectively to cultivate a more regular practice of Self-Leadership.

First of all, this book will not change your life. Quite the sales pitch, right? But after (and during) reading it, you will have access to everything you need in order to change your own life, shift your perspective, and have more effective and productive interpretations of the situations and circumstances that face you.

If you experiment with the examples, stories, and distinctions that I share throughout this book, you will instantly see the world differently, which is the first step to living your life differently.

Second, this book is not an instruction manual. There are no step-by-step processes for you to follow, nothing you have to try to agree with or believe in, no scientific studies to convince you of the validity of what I'm sharing, and no talk of a *right* or a *wrong* way to be.

If anything, this book is a *destruction* manual—breaking down the self-imposed walls and barriers that I worked so tirelessly to erect over the first few decades of my life. In fact, it will read more like a private diary of personal reminders than a traditional, advice-filled, step-by-step self-help book.

This is the book that I needed to read (and will no doubt refer to for the rest of my life for a gentle reminder or forty) to help me see through the lies, myths, and fundamental misunderstandings I held for so long about how the world worked. (Spoiler: It never seemed to "work" for me until I developed this new understanding; this new truth.)

Lastly, this book is not a *shame guide*. We will talk about this later in the chapter called "Deep Shame Thrombosis." Until then, know that it is not for you to read through and then beat yourself up for all the ways you've been a Prisoner in the past. Doing that just makes

you a Prisoner of your *Prisoner-ness*! It is a double-whammy that doesn't serve you.

I invite you to set the intention as you read this book that a *Prison Break* is not nearly as big and daunting as it sounds. It isn't reserved for big Hollywood blockbusters or criminal masterminds who chip away at the cement walls of their cells with a shaved down toothbrushes for 20 years. It is a seemingly small, but massively transformational event that occurs moment by moment when you open up to this new awareness, tap into your response-ability, and choose to come from the stance and innate inner power of a Self-Leader more frequently.

Without being asked for anything in return, we have been given the power of a level of intelligence and consciousness that no other being on this planet has. We can misuse this power; waste the talent, the abilities, and the opportunities for growth that are all around us; and let life *use us*. Or we can step fully into this power; become leaders in our lives, owners of our spirit, and conductors of our energy; and *use life* instead.

You now have everything you need to become a true Leader of Self, to take full ownership of what the rest of your life will look like, starting right now, if you make the choice to do so and are willing to experiment with what you will read in the pages that follow.

I've occupied the guards, I've cut power to the fences, I've unlocked the cell doors, and I've slipped you a copy of your escape route to freedom.

Let the Prison Break begin!

Started from the Bottom

Most people see the world as a threatening place, and, because they do, the world turns out, indeed, to be a threatening place.

—Paulo Coelho

What if I told you that this was the only chapter you had to read in the entire book to know the secret to Self-Leadership?

And what if I told you that what you will read is not even something I wrote?

And what if I told you that the person who did write it was a teenage girl in high school?

Well, it is (sort of), and I didn't, and she did.

With all of that in mind, take a minute to read the poem below entitled "Worst Day Ever?" by Chanie Gorkin.

Today was the absolute worst day ever
And don't try to convince me that
There's something good in every day
Because, when you take a closer look,
This world is a pretty evil place.
Even if
Some goodness does shine through once in a while
Satisfaction and happiness don't last.
And it's not true that
It's all in the mind and heart
Because
True happiness can be attained
Only if one's surroundings are good
It's not true that good exists
I'm sure you can agree that
The reality
Creates
My attitude
It's all beyond my control
And you'll never in a million years hear me say
Today was a very good day

Is it just me, or after reading this did you also immediately feel a sense of heaviness and compassion for the massive amounts of black nail polish and therapy Chanie's parents are going to have to pay for as she gets older?

I know what you are probably thinking right now. For being the only chapter in the book you need to read to understand the distinction and choice between a Self-Leader and Prisoner mindset, it isn't exactly the most uplifting thing in the world, is it?

It is our initial reaction to seeing this poem as something sad or upsetting that perfectly illustrates the way we see the world when coming from the perspective of a Prisoner. It isn't because we are stupid or hopeless, but simply because we have, for most of our lives, been conditioned to see, process, and explain things in a single way. This way is outside-in, letting our experience of the world be colored, for better or for worse, by a set of circumstances—or in this case, a sequence of words from a teenager.

We were never taught in school, and are truly lucky if we picked up from our parents or friends, that creativity is greater than circumstance—that is, our ability to use a creative approach to how we explain and interpret events and thoughts (instead of accepting them at face value based on our conditioned instant reaction mechanism) are the keys to freedom and joy.

The shift to living as a Self-Leader starts with taking what is in front of you and seeing where there is an interpretation, a perspective, or a creative remixing of the facts (remember, this is not about being delusional or pretending that reality doesn't exist) that leads to a more purposeful and productive way of feeling and being in the world.

You are going to experience just how powerful that shift can be when you re-read this poem and feel a rush of inspiration, enthusiasm, and excitement for what it hides in plain sight. So take another minute now to go back and re-read the poem, but this time, start from the bottom and read to the top.

Do you see what happened there?

You didn't need to do any deep work, dig into your past, or remember a 5-step formula to experience the freedom and happiness

that came from the small shift in how you approached the same poem that drained your spirit and optimism just moments ago.

The more you practice being open to a slight shift in perspective and a gentle guiding of your thoughts to find the gifts in all of the situations you encounter—and there are plenty of opportunities to do that throughout the rest of the book—the more this creative way of being will become a more natural and default response in your life.

How to Increase Your Chances of Winning the Lottery

> A man will be imprisoned in a room with a door that's unlocked and opens inwards; as long as it does not occur to him to pull rather than push.
>
> —Ludwig Wittgenstein

A man named John finds himself in serious financial strife.

John has always been a man of hope and faith, so he prays to his God, in the deepest and most sincere way he knows how, for help to become free from the burden of his money struggles.

"God, I need your help! I'm going to lose my house. My family and I will be homeless, and I do not know where else to turn. If you could make me win the lottery, all of our problems would be solved!"

Lottery night comes, but sadly, John is not the winner.

Things quickly start to spiral down. John gets laid off from his job, the home is foreclosed on and, to make things even worse, his wife leaves him and takes their two children with her. After each traumatic experience in this series of unfortunate events, John pleads with God to let him win the lottery, but he never does.

Finally, broke, hungry, and living out of his car, he tries again. "God, please, my life is a wreck. I have no food, no home, and no family. Please, I implore you, let me win the lottery just this once so that I can turn my life around!"

Suddenly, a flash of light rips and rumbles in the sky, and the voice of God echoes down from the heavens. "John, meet me halfway. Buy a ticket."

How many of us have lived just like "John" at one point or another? We settle into, are defeated by, or wait for someone to save us from the *circumstances* in our lives. I certainly have, but only for the better part of three decades. Please don't feel inferior or jealous if you didn't develop to the level of Prisoner mastery that I did.

Why was the answer for "John," and so many of us, to default to being a Prisoner? Why do we spend so much time and energy secretly, or vocally, requiring that someone or something outside of us makes things happen for us or creates our desired outcome? Why do we sometimes decide that life is using us and that circumstances have become an acceptable reason to live our lives with a constant feeling of powerlessness?

As you have already started to see, the powerful distinction I am most passionate about sharing and teaching in my keynote speaking, corporate training, and private coaching work is of seeing and speaking about our lives as *Self-Leaders* vs. *Prisoners*.

As a quick refresher, Self-Leaders are people who own their interpretations and responses to outside circumstances. Regardless of the specific situation, Self-Leaders see circumstances as conditions of the game of life—something to play and improv with. Prisoners, on the other hand, believe they are helpless, powerless victims—bystanders manipulated and held back by the cruel, cold world.

For example, maybe you or somebody you know (I would never ask you to out yourself), have experienced these *undeniable truths* and *circumstances* from the Prisoner mindset:

"I would love to have more quality time with my family, but my job is just too demanding."

"I'm so sick of doing work that I don't enjoy; it's too bad I don't have experience in another industry."

"I'd love to be in a committed relationship, b ut n o matter how many dates I go on, I meet nothing but boring, unmotivated deadbeats!"

And it's not just the stressful events that get blamed on circumstances. *Lucky* or positive events latch onto the *blessings* of circumstance too: "I hit my quota this month. Thank goodness the economy has finally started to bounce back!"

Behind these seemingly innocent, but concrete, statements is a sense of detachment of personal power.

Each person who leans upon circumstance, for better or worse, has given up the possibility that there is something inside of them that is responsible for their experience.

But how do you argue with circumstance? I mean, jobs can be demanding. Experience can be paramount when you want to switch

careers. Finding a mate can be a big challenge. People feeling better about the economy has to have some effect on the money they spend, right?

I'll play along. Let's assume that all of these things are true.

Here is where the shift from Prisoner to Self-Leader occurs, with a simple, two-word question. A question that I regularly pose to the people I coach (and one my coach has asked me on more occasions than I can count): *Now what?*

Our reaction to that question tells us everything we need to know about our current state of being.

If I ask someone that question, and as a response their wheels are turning, their creative juices are flowing, and we can start a highly-spirited brainstorming session, I know they are stepping into the power of Self-Leadership and courageous personal responsibility. Self-Leaders know the significance and impact of being resourceful over having resources, which is why "Now what?" is such a powerful question for them.

Sometimes, though, the reaction I get instead is one you would expect if you ordered a gluten-free quinoa and tofu smoothie from an Alabama Bar-B-Que joint.

Their head tilts sideways, they furrow their brows, and the question just doesn't register. That tells me that they still see themselves as the violently trembling, weakly rooted tree, standing out in the forest, all by itself, as a raging hurricane rips through the sky tearing it apart leaf by leaf, and limb by limb. They hunker down, close up tight, and hope and pray (like "John") that they will be protected and left standing once the big bad wind has moved on to its next powerless Prisoner. And they do it over and over and over again.

I'm speaking from experience here. For a long time, I met every circumstance with firmly clasped hands and tightly closed eyes and whispering hopeful affirmations to myself. Or I just blamed the person or thing in closest proximity to me who would be least likely to call me on my BS.

There are alternatives here, and they are what eventually occur when the "Now what?" question meets a willing and open host. The alternatives are awareness and choice. Awareness of what the circumstances are, why we give them so much power and ultimately slowing down enough to inquire and challenge our beliefs about them is what will allow more ease in choosing our response to those circumstances going forward.

The word *circumstance* comes from the Latin *circum*, meaning "around," and *stare*, which means "stand." Do you see what just happened there? The origin of *circumstance* is literally "stand around." And isn't that the exact thing we have been talking about?

When we are Prisoners of circumstance, we are in fact making the choice to *stand around*. We stand around waiting for someone to save the day, to make something happen for us, to give us the answers, to change the environment or the players or the entire game!

There is no intentionality or purpose when we are standing around. There is only passivity, hope (not to be confused with optimism, which is a very active way of being), reliance, trust, expectations, and disappointments.

"I hope that either my job becomes less demanding or that my family becomes okay with not seeing me as often."

"I trust that, at some point, a better job will come along so I can finally leave this place."

"I pray that the perfect partner effortlessly falls in my lap, and we live happily ever after!"

"I expect that since it's a new year, there will be more in my customers' budgets to buy my products and services."

There is one very big assumption present in this Prisoner understanding—that *self-initiated, self-directed action* is either unavailable or pointless. And when that assumption becomes a belief, the only thing left to lean on is circumstance. The only way to proceed is to stand around and wait.

If at this point, you are ready to choose *creation from the inside*, instead of *reaction to the outside*, you can stop reading now and start testing your new tools.

As the late psychologist Nathaniel Branden once said, "You can't leave a place you've never been." Once you see the way a Prisoner views the world and how simple the alternative approach is, it will be enough to show you the path to freedom without me telling you anything else to do.

But if you want or feel like you need to dive a little deeper into what keeps us as Prisoners in the land of circumstance in order to loosen its grip on you, please, read on.

I'm Just an Innocent Bystander...

If the Latin lesson about circumstance = standing around didn't help you make the connection to an alternate, more powerful way of being, then the concept of the *bystander* will help.

Take the example of a fiery car crash. Whether you have witnessed accidents in person or heard stories of them on the news, there are countless occurrences of vehicle collisions, trapped motorists, and

the harrowing tales of regular, everyday people who jump into action and save complete strangers from certain death.

There are two types of people in those situations. There are the ones who leap into the fire (literally and figuratively) despite the very real danger that awaits them. And then there are the bystanders.

This is not a book on morality, ethics, or selflessness; I'm not concerned with that right now. I am simply using this analogy because most of us know exactly which category we (think we) would step into in that type of situation.

My belief is that many of the reasons bystanders choose to be bystanders are the same reasons that we choose our dependence on circumstances instead of exercising Self-Leadership in our lives.

"I'm Afraid..."

The first reason, fear, is a no-brainer. The difference, though, between the fear that a fledgling Self-Leader encounters versus what the bystanders of a fiery car wreck must overcome is that only the bystanders at the crash site face the potential for real danger. There is no real, tangible threat in exercising Self-Leadership, only an opportunity for growth.

It can seem scary no longer to blame something outside of you for how you feel and instead take full ownership and personal responsibility. Believe me; I experienced this first hand when I first started practicing the transition from Prisoner to Self-Leader! Because if it isn't their fault that you are where you are now (or that you aren't where you want to be), whose fault is it?

But here is the thing about fault: When you choose and practice Self-Leadership, fault disappears. I don't mean the assignment of fault; I mean the actual idea of fault itself ceases to exist.

Let's travel back in time to childhood for a second. I've learned that some of the most powerful recollections of innocence and Self-Leadership come from our time as children.

When we were children, we knew exactly what we wanted, and we typically threw tantrums when our captors, er, I mean caretakers tested our innate sense of Self-Leadership.

So imagine that, as a child, you pushed a little racecar across the living room floor. In its path was the leg of a piece of furniture, and the car crashed into it.

Who would you blame?

...the car for not being aware enough to change its direction?

...the furniture for not being respectful of your desire to play and get out of the way?

...yourself for pushing the car with that amount of force or for not surveying the land beforehand to make sure its path would be unobstructed?

As a child, you would never waste time with any of that. I don't mean that you would think those things and then decide not to assign fault or blame. It is simply that those ideas would not even occur to you.

What would you do instead?

You would likely go over to the couch leg where the racecar lay, pick it up and, without missing a beat, use that piece of furniture as your new home base to operate from. And this time, I bet the

car would "learn" to fly. This is a simple reminder and example of the "Now what?" question, one of the Self-Leaders' super simple secret weapons.

As we remove blame and fault from our toolkit, we are able to take ownership of how we respond (instead of react) to the situations we face. We can start to approach our scary and uncomfortable experiences from a place of creative action, tapping into our best selves and choosing to bring that part of us out at any given moment.

There is no real fear in letting go of attachment to circumstances, only the promise of a new and more effective perspective that you get to own and practice as the innovative, creative, and empowered version of yourself.

"I Don't Know How to..."

Another reason that bystanders sit on the sideline and Prisoners cling to outside influence is based on the belief that they don't know how to do anything differently.

Sometimes bystanders at an accident scene will become active once they see someone else step up. Once they have a frame of reference for what it looks like to jump into action and help those in need. The parallel for choosing Self-Leadership is that many of us have never seen this choice (remember, Self-Leadership is a choice, not a part of our character) modeled. It seems too foreign or too daunting to leap out and try on our own for the first time. What if we do it wrong? What if we fail? What if we are just destined to be Prisoners forever?

If you are starting to get the language of people in Prisoner mode, you will have caught the irony in that last statement. You can now see the reality in the *how to* dilemma you think you are facing.

I too had the same questions about making this shift because it all seemed like a foreign language to me.

Choice? Choosing to be a Self-Leader? I didn't get it. You may as well have been speaking Aramaic with a Scottish accent. Thankfully, I had the guidance, support, and wisdom of my confidant and mentor Steve Chandler to help introduce me to this way of being and reinforce that it is simply a moment-by-moment, day-by-day practice.

If you have never had a frame of reference for this type of life leadership from parents, friends, teachers, bosses, coaches, mentors, etc., well guess what? You have one now! Me!

My transition into choosing to see and speak about the world as a Self-Leader instead of a Prisoner was a major turning point in my life.

This book will act as a reminder to myself about the power of choice and taking responsibility for creating my reality and experiences in this world in the inevitable periods where I will need a refresher of this exact message. Remember, it is a moment-by-moment practice.

You don't *finish* Self-Leadership anymore than Michael Jordan *finished* practicing his jump shot or Steve Jobs *finished* practicing innovation.

Just like you don't go from the couch to being a marathon runner overnight, it is the consistency of challenging your thoughts, testing new actions, and playing the game of Self-Leadership that anchors it and makes it easier to access going forward.

If the people who do become marathon runners miss a day and slide back a bit, they can simply choose to go running the next day

without losing any real progress toward their goals. If you have a *Prisoner moment*, it is simply a data point, a reminder to say to yourself, "Cool, I chose to be a Prisoner in that situation. No biggie, what do I choose *next*?"

In the chapters to come, you will see tons of examples of "Now what?" and "What do I choose next?" in practice.

For now, just know that your time as a bystander and fearful Prisoner is done. You have been the hero of your story, a powerful Self-Leader and creator, since day one. It may have taken you 10,000 days (give or take a few thousand) to uncover it, but today is the only one of those days that matters. Because this is the day you choose to start playing a new game where you choose to tap into your best self and highest quality of thinking moment-by-moment—from a place of enthusiasm, gentleness, excellence and a spirit of mastery.

No lottery ticket needed.

Your Life Is Not a Correctional Facility

Become a possibilitarian. No matter how dark things seem to be or actually are, raise your sights and see the possibilities-always see them, for they're always there.

—Norman Vincent Peale

When I start coaching someone, it doesn't take long to see whether their default interpretation of the circumstances in their world come from the place of Prisoner or Self-Leader. I pay attention to their language, their perspective, and their explanations for why they aren't living the way they say they desire to live. I listen to their excuses and misunderstandings, not as an omniscient, enlightened guru who has all the answers, but instead as if I were reminiscing, experiencing a sense of nostalgia of just how shackled of a Prisoner I was for the first 30 years of my life.

The Prisoner mentality is not the only thing we once had in common though. The other belief that they often still hold when we begin our work together is that they need to be *fixed* in order to make the shift from Prisoner to Self-Leader.

I know exactly what that feels like because it is how I felt when I started doing this work on myself a number of years ago. It's a feeling that I was somehow living the wrong way.

I remember feeling like I was in desperate need of remediation and rehabilitation. Committing to my own evolution meant my life had become one long stint in a correctional facility, and if I was able to learn the lessons on how I should be living, then and only then, I would have a chance to be released early for good behavior.

But we are not inmates, and we were not designed to be confined. Transformation does not involve a proverbial corrections officer walking down the halls with a baton, smacking it against the jail cell bars to back us down until we learn the errors of our ways and become productive citizens. This is, by definition, just another example of the Prisoner mindset.

We think we must change our perspective by force, through shame or guilt, or out of compliance, and only then will we somehow become free of our self-imposed restraints forever. But we are not meant to live our lives that way. We are far too creative, far too capable, and far too mighty, especially once we access and activate the powerful Self-Leaders inside of us that have been there all along.

Instead of being militant and overly serious about my own evolution and the growth and possibilities of the people I train and coach, I want to approach the process with the love, innovation, and creativity of an incubator.

There are two different types of incubators that I am familiar with, and both can be powerful reminders of a more effective, Self-Leader-based approach to taking ownership of what we want to create in our world. Both are devoid of the limitations and disheartening discouragement of *growth by punishment*.

The first type of incubator is one that underweight babies are placed in shortly after birth. I don't have any direct experience with these as it is rumored that I came out of the womb pleasantly plump with a Snickers bar and a funnel cake. But for those who have been in them, the incubator creates an environment within the apparatus that helps them to be nourished, grow stronger, and have constant and unconditional support around them.

We would never accuse the babies of having done something wrong to be in the incubator, and they don't need to be fixed or forced into change. It is simply understood that the incubator is the best place for them to be right now in order to grow stronger and healthier, and become the mentally and physically tough humans that we all know they are capable of being; the ones that we can see inside of them even if it isn't evident to the rest of the world, or the babies, yet.

The other type of incubator that I love to think about is one that I have had direct experience with—business incubators.

I launched my first startup inside of a business incubator, and it was a place where my business partners and I received love, guidance, mentorship, training, and advocacy. We weren't stupid or wrong or broken when we applied to be accepted into this exclusive program.

In fact, it was quite the opposite. Business incubators typically only accept companies that have a lot of potential—those who want to grow and see the process of growth as fun and exciting.

It isn't for businesses that are struggling and need someone to fix them. Instead, it exists as a way to pour attention and creativity into helping these entrepreneurs build the best version of themselves and their companies.

Allow yourself to see any work you do in shifting from Prisoner to Self-Leader with this same creative approach.

Nothing is wrong with you, and nothing *has to* change.

But if there is something in your life that doesn't feel like its working as well as you'd like it to, and you want to explore a potentially more effective way of seeing the world around you, Self-Leadership is the answer!

Treat it like an experiment, a scavenger hunt where instead of searching for trinkets, you are exploring the landscape of your world for new ways of *being* to try on and new ways of *doing* to test out. Those opportunities are boundless and hidden in plain sight at every turn.

Build an incubator for your possibilities and potential, make it the most fun and creative game you've ever played, and watch what grows out of it—what you are capable of creating.

You Weren't Born to Be Anything

The self is not something ready-made, but something in continuous formation through choice of action.

—John Dewey

One fundamental misunderstanding that I clung to tightly when I first started my journey of courage and personal responsibility was that people who think and act as Self-Leaders were somehow genetically predisposed to be able to do so.

We have all heard (or said ourselves if we are being honest) that he or she is naturally "take charge" or "heroic," or has that "special something" that we just don't have! For those of us who are used to explaining the world from a Prisoner mindset, this is an incredibly comforting story to believe. Because it is far easier to make excuses, beat ourselves up, or just watch the "chosen few" who were *born to*

do those things than it is to admit the truth that we all were *born to choose* those things.

The stories we make up about ourselves and others are very powerful—for better or for worse. Thinking, saying, or living from the belief that "I can't because…" or "They can because…" immediately removes the power of who you can be(come) in order to protect and secure who you believe you are.

But the truth is, you are *nothing*!

I know that sounds harsh, but what I mean is that there is nothing permanent or pervasive about your way of being, your personality, your character traits, or your ability to create, inside and out.

Saying that you are or are not a certain way is a death sentence for growth and happiness. It is carving your initials in quick drying cement that, once set, will always and forever limit your potential.

You are not that fixed persona, though. You have no limit on the awareness you can develop, the person you can become, and the choices you can make regardless of any past personality, performance, or perspectives that have been present.

We are all born with an equal ability to be, do, and create anything we can conceive of. The difference is whether we choose to exercise it or not. While some realize that sooner than others, how long it has taken to "get it" means nothing—thank goodness, since it was about three decades for me; the only thing that matters is what we do with the awareness once we have it.

I had a mantra almost my entire adult life that went like this: "That's just the way I am." When someone cut me off in traffic, and I chased them down, the reason was simple. I was an angry person— "That's just the way I am." When someone would criticize me, I

would lash out or shut down. Again, the rationale was sound; I just reacted without any regard for how much damage my explosion would cause—"That's just the way I am."

Once I realized that "That's just the way I am" was not the powerful conviction I once thought it was, and I got in touch with my creative abilities to choose a way of being that brought me peace and freedom instead of stress and anger, the whole world started to open up. I finally saw the gifts of creation I had at my disposal, the gifts to be whoever I wanted to be at any given moment.

Once you see this for yourself, which can happen instantly, your world will never be the same. Through awareness, response-ability, and choice, you will experience that you have all of the gifts you need to become a true leader of self, and those gifts don't expire until you do.

Which Train of Thought Will You Board?

Thoughts are just what is. They appear. They're innocent. They're not personal. They're like the breeze or the leaves on the trees or the raindrops falling. Thoughts arise like that, and we can make friends with them. Would you argue with a raindrop?

—Byron Katie

I'm sure you have heard the term *train of thought* before—a stream of consciousness, a seemingly self-propelled mechanism of thinking.

Trains of thought occur much like any other thinking, without us trying to make it so. We hear or see something, remember or process something, respond to or react to something—and suddenly and

without notice, we are launched out of the station with the speed and velocity of a bullet train!

When the train's cargo is full of creativity, enthusiasm, fun, and novelty, we are happy to enjoy the ride. We even throw our hands up and yell *faster, faster*!

But what about when the train is instead filled with anxiety, stress, debilitating mental chatter, and self-imposed limitations? Suddenly an otherwise adventurous journey becomes a soul-sucking, spirit-crushing hell ride through darkness and despair. Think Willy Wonka and the psychedelic boat trip without the promise of candy!

Where we often get ourselves into trouble is when we forget that a train of thought operates much the same way that a real train does. It is simply a vehicle that has no effect on us unless you decide to board it.

There are an unlimited number of both positive and negative trains of thought with plenty of open seats and departure times scheduled at every single moment. The thoughts that reside in each of these trains are not forced or bestowed upon you because you are not the train, and you are not those thoughts; they exist independently of you.

You are the holder of a universal boarding pass. You can step back and see the two different trains on the tracks, facing opposite directions, and you own the power to choose which one you will board. It is that choice that leads to the decision of which thoughts you will take on as your own.

Prolific author, godfather of coaching, and my homeboy-for-life Steve Chandler made this crystal clear for me when he once told me: "If you can see a train pulling out of the station, you are not on that

train. If you can see your thought, you are not your thought; you are what sees it."

A key element of Self-Leadership is the understanding that we do not have to become Prisoners of our thoughts—especially the ones we didn't create to begin with, the ones that just mysteriously appear in our minds and that we think we must fight off with a big wooden stick.

We can instead choose to love the thoughts that occur to us, welcome them without resistance, and since we are not attaching to or making them significant, we can watch with fondness as they board the train and destination for which they are destined. As we bid them farewell, wave lovingly, and allow the train to fade into the distance, we are now free to choose new thinking, to board a new train of thought that truly serves us. With that choice, we create the moment-by-moment experience of our lives.

slick = skilled
smooth job
flat expert
clear
plain

What If You Stopped Chasing Your Dreams?

I am my own experiment.
I am my own work of art.

—Madonna Ciccone

Chase or follow or (insert verb here) your dreams!

It is probably one of the first messages they teach you in "motivational speaker" school. I wouldn't know; they rejected me as soon as I submitted my application and essay about how much I loved cloudy, cold, rainy days. They don't take kindly to that kind of morbid sophistication. *Perfection*

Unhealthy

smooth But when I think about chasing something, anything, whether the slick pickpocket who is running away with my wallet, an elevator inhabited by people who seem immune to my cries of "hold that door" or the buy-one-get-one-free Starbucks coupon that slipped out of my hands and is being carried down the street by that

almost comically placed gust of wind—chasing feels like me trying to overcome an outside circumstance that is preventing me from having what I want.

avoid
"/us/"   So why would I want to give my dreams and aspirations any *of our wishes* chance to elude me? Why would I put myself in a situation where I have to hope that my pickpocket trips on uneven pavement, that I sprint fast enough to catch the elevator door sensor, or that an unsuspecting stranger steps on and saves my coupon?

What if, instead of being a Prisoner to this thing outside of you that requires you to cross your fingers tight, hunt it down, or try to sneak up behind it and tackle it, there was a more fun and less stressful way to succeed?

What if the things you want to attain—love, money, health, etc.—were not something outside of you that you needed to sub- or unconsciously attract, but were instead things you consciously chose to create?

If I truly want to be a creator of wealth, health, and rock-solid relationships, I don't want to be passive in that quest.

I want to be active.

I want to be fully engaged and purposeful—the creator and interpreter of my circumstances, not the helpless Prisoner of some elusive "success wizard" that only waves his magic wand over people he thinks deserve his gifts!

I'm not against affirmations or visualization or vision boards. I think all of those things can be fun and playful, and help improve your mindset and the strength of your desires. Heck, if you follow me on social media, you will know that I am, myself, a quote junkie!

مرابطا سيُمستكبر

What I want to add to the mix is a high level of diligent, aligned, sincere, purposeful action to the equation.

hard .
working
Tireless

I want to be a verb.

I recognize that my life is much more of an Etch-a-Sketch than a stone tablet. I experiment playfully and, if the time comes that I want to reinvent and try something new, I just shake it up and start drawing a new picture.

As a Self-Leader, you don't waste time trying to find artists outside of yourself to draw your masterpiece for you. Where's the fun in that?

Instead, you engage the wellspring of joyful and creative energy that comes from giving up the chase, slowing down, enjoying the perfection of the present moment and playfully exploring and experimenting with the limitless opportunities you create for yourself.

Your Intuition Is Drunk

> *Most people believe the mind to be a mirror, more or less accurately reflecting the world outside them, not realizing on the contrary that the mind is itself the principal element of creation.*
>
> —Rabindranath Tagore

I am probably going to get my soul-centered, innate-wisdom card revoked for this one, but I have some beef with intuition.

Not since the late 1800s has the word *intuition* been so prevalent in our society as it is today. It is this intangible sense from which we can ask for answers and then listen and trust it to find peace, happiness, and success. It is often spoken about and believed to be an infallible inner voice that knows all, sees all, and gives us surefire direction for anything we may be unsure, uncertain, or uneasy about. Sounds great, right?

Maybe I am jaded because I have been "steered wrong" or felt worse as a result of listening to my intuition in the past and so now I'm condemning any usefulness in the practice. Stick with me for a few minutes, though—there is a little more to that story.

I consider myself a *spiritual pragmatist* (I wanted to find something as pompous and pretentious sounding as possible—did it work?). What that means is I believe in a source, a higher power, spirit or whatever you want to call it. At the same time, I believe in our ability to massage, interpret, imagine, and create what we do with what that spirit provides us, as well as being honest about from where those messages are born.

Now, I know this is going to contradict the essence of "intuition," but I want to invite you to view intuition as something *outside* of you just for the sake of discussion.

Let's say that instead of it being an inner voice, that intuition is your most trusted friend, your favorite uncle, your college advisor, your coach, or the best boss you ever had. They have never steered you wrong. They always have your best interest at heart.

But what if one day, when you were in need of some guidance, you went to them for help, advice, or support, and you found them sloppy drunk! If the intoxicated version of this person doesn't resonate with you or you are easily offended, then let's just say that on this particular day they are in a low place, challenged by major stresses, sick with the flu—essentially not "themselves."

They would never say no to talking to you when you need them, so you approach them as you always have, but the result of what you get from that encounter feels different. It is not grounded in the same high-spirited, possibility-based, creation-centered place that

it normally is. Do you trust their counsel and direction in the same way that you normally would?

Most likely not. But that is exactly what I have seen my clients and myself do when we ask a source (ourselves) with diminished capacity (caught up in our thinking and in a low state of mind) for help and then become a Prisoner to their (our) suggestions.

If you really encountered someone like this, you wouldn't think twice about discarding the advice. You would recognize that this person who has been so selflessly caring toward you and so committed to being there for you in the past, no matter what, needs some compassion and love *from* you right now.

The dependability, truthfulness, and power of your intuition are directly related to your state of mind and quality of thinking.

Decreased consciousness, high stress, and low spirits = *drunk intuition* (it looks the same at first glance, but once it opens its mouth, you can tell it is a complete stranger).

Noticing this drunkenness is a gift. It can be your spiritual early warning system signaling that something needs to change before you ask the questions you need answers to. You can't force someone who is drunk to be sober instantly or someone who is down to be up instantly, so when this occurs, it simply means that now is not the time to ask. It also means that a bit of self-love and self-compassion is the best thing for you.

After leaving my last corporate position, I launched multiple companies, pitched investors, and tried to sell to and service clients, all while trying to stay upbeat, positive and creative for myself, my family, and my business partners. I would often wait until I was in a low quality of thinking to ask my intuition if this was the path I should be or stay on. There were more times than I can count where

I'd sit searching job listings on the Internet, heavy with stress and despair over the unknowns of the future.

During these times, I would ask my inner guidance if I should stop all of this *business owner nonsense,* and my drunk intuition would come stumbling in, spilling its 30-year-old scotch, slurring its words, and saying *"Yeah, this is dumb; just get a job. Do you know how safe and secure and lurkative that would be?"* (lurkative was my drunk intuition's attempt at saying "lucrative" by the way).

I finally stopped this cycle when I gained the insight that there was a direct connection between how I was feeling and the quality of my thoughts.

From this understanding, it became much easier to recognize when I needed to hold off asking my inner Prisoner for advice and instead allow my calm, conscious and courageous Self-Leader to reemerge. I did this through acknowledging the heavy emotions and the thoughts I was caught up in and gently letting them pass —like clouds in the sky or products moving along on a conveyor belt. I didn't need to interfere, as they were fully capable of leaving on their own—as they always do naturally, unless we attach to them and slow down their departure.

This awareness helps me to remember not to ask for answers from my inner knowing when I'm fairly certain that it couldn't pass a proverbial Breathalyzer test or would ruin the joy of a petting zoo at a kids' birthday party with its *Debbie Downer* demeanor.

On the flip side of drunk intuition: relaxed, creative, high-spirited, and best self = innovative, problem-solving, clear, and loving intuition. This is where Self-Leaders thrive because their

mental health allows their hearts and heads to speak without all of the noise and confusion that was previously muddying the waters.

In fact, when it comes to shifting from being a Prisoner to a Self-Leader, I have started to replace the word *intuition* with another word that I believe is rooted in possibilities and action. It is a word that primes us to be more creative and to bring more courage to our challenges.

The word is *illumination.* Clarification - Simplification

Isn't that what we are looking for when we ask for a spirit or God or Mother Nature or our intellect and inner-knowing to assist?

Are we not seeking for light to be shined on the murky, shadowy, or tangled uncertainty that we feel is holding us back from experiencing some deeper form of happiness or fulfillment?

If so, then let's convert the noun *illumination* into a verb that we can use to shift ourselves into a creative form of intuitive interpretation. You can practice this by taking any answer you receive from your intuition and then asking yourself this question: *"How can I use the answer I received to illuminate an opportunity I may not have seen previously?"*

If your answer to that question is that you can't, it may just mean that you are not yet in a high-spirited, creative place (a.k.a. drunk intuition), which is completely okay. It doesn't make you wrong or stupid; it just means you aren't in the most effective space, in that moment, to handle the situation in the most productive way.

The answer is to slow down and acknowledge and welcome whatever thoughts are occurring in that moment and not to try to overcome them by shame, force, or resistance. Trying to force yourself to act sober will never be as effective as allowing yourself to simply *sober up* naturally.

When I allow my mind to relax and calm down, I can be more creative about the meaning of the messages I receive. From this place, opportunities that I otherwise never would have seen are illuminated.

Let's go back to my example about asking my intuition if I should get a regular job instead of continuing to follow the more challenging path of entrepreneurship when I was already feeling low. When my intuition responded, *"Yes, get a job! This shouldn't be this hard; maybe you just aren't cut out for it,"* it didn't illuminate anything. In fact, the opposite happened; everything felt heavier and darker. That was my cue instead to chill out, relax, and focus on raising my level of consciousness before asking for guidance or direction.

I wonder if this was the rationale behind the "Ask again later" response on the old Magic 8 Ball fortune-telling toy. Who knew that a cheap tchotchke with a 20-sided die floating in a blue-dyed liquid could be so insightful?

In this particular example of whether or not to continue on my entrepreneurial journey, something very interesting happened. Once I had improved my inner stance and my consciousness had increased, the question of whether or not to continue pursuing my path disappeared. I no longer needed to ask or answer that question.

If I had still felt the desire to answer the question once my quality of mind had increased, it might have illuminated an opportunity to ask for more support from my business partners. Or it could have reminded me that I needed to be more patient or make sure I was practicing self-care with my meditation, eating, exercise, and sleep schedule.

There is always something trying to emerge in conflict and discomfort. There is a gift in every thought, even if it seems impossible to see when we are caught up in our thinking in the moment.

Powerful answers from an intuition of a solid, sober, Self-Leader will illuminate opportunities to be, feel, have, and create whatever you want in your world. This is the place where fears and negative self-talk, although they may show up, won't be able to dominate the conversation. Here they are met with understanding and compassion instead of clenched fists and a vendetta of destruction.

Self-Leadership invites you to be active in the illumination and interpretation of the messages you receive and to test those meanings for yourself instead of simply trying to believe in them. It asks that you rely more on your imagination and ability for creation than the false limitations that you have been taught, or convinced exist.

Consider viewing intuition through the lens of this quote by Albert Einstein: *"When I examine myself and my methods of thought, I come close to the conclusion that the gift of imagination has meant more to me than any talent for absorbing absolute knowledge."*

You cannot be beat (up) from this imaginative place because the light will push out the dark, illumination will outshine limitation, and inspiration will trump expiration, but only always!

Show Up and Dance

> When you come to the edge of all the light
> you have, and must take a step into the
> darkness of the unknown, believe that one
> of two things will happen. Either there will be
> something solid for you to stand on
> —or you will be taught how to fly.
>
> —Patrick Overton

During a coaching session with one of my clients, Nathaniel, we were talking about the debilitating fear of uncertainty that can surface when we decide to (or decide to decide to—how's that for new age double-talk) make a change in our lives. And while it looks like fear, smells like fear, and tastes like fear (which in my mind resembles bad gas station sushi), what we are really feeling is varying degrees of discomfort.

As we dove a little deeper into this idea, Nathaniel had a powerful insight. Nathaniel is a special guy for lots of reasons, one of which is his background in improvisational theater a.k.a. *improv comedy*.

Can you imagine the level of discomfort and uncertainty you would feel if you were to go on stage, in front of a group of people, and it was impossible to prepare at all? I think most people would opt for the gas station sushi!

But in revisiting his past improv experiences, Nathaniel shared with me this gem: *"The victory in improv is simply showing up!"*

In other words, since certainty is not available in any form, and there are no guarantees as to what will happen before, during, or after the performance, all you can control is which parts of yourself you will bring to the stage when the show starts.

This is a beautiful metaphor for the choice between being a Prisoner and Self-Leader. In the midst of uncertainty and discomfort, we can each choose to be stressed out, get anxious, and shut down, or we can choose to relax, be playful, and let our natural creative intelligence do its thing.

This same powerful principle applies in every area of our lives. It may have been taught, modeled, and drilled into us that we need to have perfect information, complete certainty to get started or that having a detailed roadmap keeps us safe from something that would otherwise devastate us. But that simply isn't true.

It is the fundamental misconceptions that if we analyze meticulously enough, process deeply enough, and struggle long enough, we can protect ourselves from every unknown that exists— and the ones we make up (if I were to re-write Jay-Z's hit song "99 Problems," I would change the lyrics to "I've got 99 problems, and 99 of them are completely imaginary").

I'm not saying there is anything wrong with creating a plan, setting an intention, or having an idea of the path you would like to take. But there are two things I'll invite you to consider that will make your planning more effective.

First, we can choose whether to build our plans out of desperation and fear (Prisoner) or out of fun and possibilities (Self-Leader). The energy we bring to planning is even more important than the activity of planning itself.

And second, know that with or without a plan, we have never had certainty in any decision we have made in any part of our lives. We may think we have, and it is easy to look back on the things that "worked out" to connect the imaginary dots in order to make it look like our particular mode of analyzing and processing is what made those things successful — but it is simply not true.

What *really* happened is that we danced with the doubt.

We undulated with the uncertainty.

We did the Rumba with our reservations.

It doesn't mean that it was always easy or effortless or that it even felt like a dance. But doesn't real dancing work the same way? Anytime I dance, especially in public, it feels more like a futile attempt at defying gravity than a graceful flow of partnered movement.

Seeing the world through the lens of Self-Leadership means that while the existence of the dance may not be in our control, our response to how we show up when someone invites us out on the dance floor is!

In reality, our only guarantee is the one we make to ourselves. The one that affirms our commitment to show up and do the work —

the only things we have any influence on — without any attachment to what we think that has to look like in the end.

When we can playfully hold this intention of being high on commitment and low on attachment *(sincerely playful as I often call it)*, we are able to not only appreciate but, dare I say, enjoy every step of the dance.

Alan Watts said, *"The only way to make sense out of change is to plunge into it, move with it, and join the dance."*

Plunge…move…join…a reminder to live life as a verb, in a state of high-spirited, enjoyment-creating, not-so-serious play.

Remember, too, that there has yet to be anything you have faced in your life that you couldn't handle. I know that to be true because you are reading this right now. You are resourceful, response-able, and resilient more than you even realize.

Please don't take what I've shared with you here as an invitation to be passive or hope that visualization and detachment from *doing something* will magically create what you want.

What I'm saying is exactly the opposite: Don't worry about the steps or the exact path you will take to get from point A to point B on the dance floor. Just show up open and pay attention, be ready to play, dance your butt off, have fun, and the rest will take care of itself. That is about the closest I can get to being certain of anything, and I wouldn't have it any other way!

It's Not Your Only Line in the Play

> "I had no choice," actually means, "I had only one path that was easy in the moment."
>
> —Seth Godin

When I give keynote speeches and training on the Art of Self-Leadership, one of the questions I inevitably get during Q&A or privately after my talks is "But how can I be a Self-Leader 100% of the time?"

Unfortunately (for them), it's a question I can't answer because I don't know.

The beauty and power of reinvention and shifting from being a Prisoner to being a Self-Leader is that it is a lens through which you interpret, explain, and experience your world. It isn't a preemptive activity or something you plan for; it is a moment-by-moment decision.

→ تصور
understand درک

Prevention جلو گیری

It is a choice; one that gets easier to access the more you choose it—just like a *swear jar* that you deposit a dollar into every time you spout a colorful four-letter word to help you alleviate that vocabulary from your daily speech (What, you never had one of those? You f**kin' missed out!).

The truth is we are always making a choice, at any given moment with any given situation and with any given person, to react as Prisoners or to respond as Self-Leaders.

A more realistic question, or at least one that I can answer, is "Do you choose to respond as a Self-Leader 100% of the time to 100% of your experiences?"

My answer is simple, "Oh hell no!" In fact, if I did, I would have much less to train and teach others about.

Sometimes I do *choose* to be a Prisoner, but the difference now is that I have enough self-awareness to admit it was a choice. I also acknowledge that though I may have missed the opportunity to choose Self-Leadership in the moment that just passed, it has no bearing on me choosing Self-Leadership in this present moment or the next moment.

Something else I don't do (as much) anymore when I have a Prisoner moment is that I don't beat myself up for having reacted from a Prisoner state of mind in that moment. If I do, I'm just sinking deeper into a Prisoner perspective, being a Prisoner of my own Prisoner-ness— crying over spilt milk and then crying because I'm crying over spilt milk. That is a downward spiral that can get messy and very *Inception*-like really quickly.

Through my own experimentation and quest for mastery of Self-Leadership (and when I say "mastery," I mean in the way Michael Jordan "mastered" his jump shot. It never ended; he never stopped

practicing mastery. He never got to a point where he said, "I think I have this jump shot thing figured out, coach. From now on just call me when the game starts."), I have come to learn that having a momentary Prisoner reaction can be one of the greatest gifts I can receive.

It is in recognizing my Prisoner moments without shame, blame, or guilt that I am able to see the obvious contrast and clear distinction, both in how I felt and how I behaved, between that experience and one where I exercised Self-Leadership.

It is a chance to see that, for example, if the freshly brewed coffee burned your mouth when you tried to gulp it out of the carafe, another option is to transfer it to a cup and let it cool down and sip it instead next time. What better time is there to see that possibility than when you experienced something that is the opposite of what you would have liked to experience?

Ignoring the power of those moments and instead defaulting to the all-or-nothing mentality of a Prisoner is one of the biggest factors I have seen that derails people's practice of Self-Leadership.

They will often start off excited to learn and practice this new awareness and understanding. Then they quickly shift to the worry of having to make it be the way they will think and act forever! A single instance of Prisoner thinking or behavior gives them the evidence they need to prove that they could never reap the benefits of consistent Self-Leadership—it's just not "who they are." That absolutely asinine assumption only serves to create debilitating stress and pressure *(stressure?)* on what can otherwise be a fun practice. Then, as a natural next step, that heaviness returns them to Prisoner thinking because the inner chatter goes, "If I can't do it all the time, I'm not going to do it at all!"

It's the same reason we make the New Year's resolution to go the gym five days a week for the rest of our lives and as soon as we miss a day, we give up because, "If I can't do it all the time, I'm not going to do it at all!"

Listen, the Prisoner can be a militant, unforgiving, spiteful schmuck! So for you to have the best chance at staying consistent, relaxed, and on-purpose with your Self-Leadership practice, I want to take you through a short exercise.

Imagine for a minute that you were in a play, a live stage production where you had one small but pivotal line to deliver.

This isn't some trivial piece of dialog, blowing a horn and welcoming the king, or screaming, "RUN!" when the monster appears from stage left. This line is a highly climactic, powerful phrase that, when well-executed and delivered with confidence and charisma, will make or break the entire performance. The reviews, the applause, your entire future all rest on this one string of otherwise meaningless words.

How do you think you would feel as you emerge from the shadows, hit your mark, and begin to deliver your linguistic pièce de résistance?

Did you think of words like *relaxed, enthusiastic, effortless, unattached,* and *fun?* Probably not, but why not?

Because so much rides on this one line!

This is it. No redemption. No do-overs. No experimenting. It's *all or nothing.*

Now suppose instead that you were the lead in the play.

Imagine that you have countless scenes, pages and pages of dialog, dozens of interactions and, in one particular instance, you

flubbed a word or gesture. Might it sting a little bit? Possibly. But in the next 30 seconds, you will have another line to deliver—three shows a night for the next two weeks.

The failure or success of the previous line or previous night's performance means nothing when choosing how to deliver this next line. You can approach each line from a place of Self-Leadership and genuine love instead of fear because there is no longer a belief of scarcity or the heavy-handed, all-or-nothing Prisoner mentality to contend with, struggle against, or overcome.

There's a reason why doctors and followers of religion call what they do *practice*. Because they and anyone who exercises Self-Leadership are presented with limitless opportunities to learn, test, play, tweak, and choose their response. It is through that practice that we develop a deep knowing that we are never defined by any single moment.

As you are venturing out to start seeing and living your life as a Self-Leader more often, see that you don't just have multiple lines in the play; you have all of them!

When you really see the truth in this, it is powerful and gives you the freedom to play with and use life instead of treating each moment like it is make or break, do or die, all or nothing.

One of my favorite comedians, Demetri Martin, illuminates just how unlimited our options are to exercise Self-Leadership when he said:

My favorite fruit is grapes. Because with grapes, you always get another chance. 'Cause you know, if you have a crappy apple or a peach, you're stuck with that crappy piece of fruit. But if you have a crappy grape, no problem—just move on to the next.

Even Though "It's Not Your Only Line in the Play"

In case there was any little bit of residual Prisoner that was hanging around as you read that last chapter, I wanted to share one important note before we move forward on our Self-Leadership road trip.

Very simply put, the message in the previous chapter was "there is always next time." But that would have been too short of a chapter to pass muster with my editor.

Like other seasoned stage performers, experienced stand-up comedians are masterful with this practice. If they go up on stage for the 6:30 p.m. show, try some new jokes, and completely flop, they know that they will have another set an hour later to tweak the jokes or try out other material.

They don't entertain the thought that a 6:30 bomb equals the end of their career or the universe giving them a sign to quit or that they just aren't good enough or cut out for this career. For them, it was simply an experiment that yielded useful information that they can put into practice just one hour later to create potentially different results.

"There is always next time" speaks again to the relative impermanence of any situation. There is nothing permanent about our circumstances or about ourselves the way we see the world.

There is one caveat on this concept that I feel is my responsibility to share.

"There is always next time" is reserved for those who are in action, not for the bystanders. It is a reward for the zealous re-inventers and experimenters, a reminder to keep playing the game.

The Prisoner-minded are not to use it as an excuse to wait to take action now because "there is always next time." It is not a mental snooze button that says, "I don't feel like it. Maybe next time." We are not to use it as emotional hot cocoa to keep us comfy and wrapped in a cocoon of inactivity, fear, and doubt.

It is a powerful war cry, an exclamation, a high-spirited recommitment to exercising our creativity and staying active in the process of reinvention, regardless of the outcome.

"There is always next time" is the permission we give ourselves to stay both vigilant and playful, to keep the devotion and discipline of a professional and the enthusiasm and novelty of an amateur.

Quieting the Baby Assassin

As long as you think that the cause of your problem is "out there"—as long as you think that anyone or anything is responsible for your suffering—the situation is hopeless. It means that you are forever in the role of victim, that you've suffering in paradise.

—Byron Katie

It was 2011, but I still remember it like it was yesterday. I was lying in my hospital bed. The anesthesiologist was prepping my left arm, and my loving and concerned Jewish mother was standing at the foot of the bed. I was about to undergo bariatric weight loss surgery after a year of physical and mental preparation for one of the boldest and most drastic decisions I had made in my life, for my life.

As the sleepy juice started to kick in—no turning back now—my mom looked into my slightly loopy eyes and said with all of the sincerity in the world, "Are you sure you really want to do this?"

"What?! Seriously, Mom!" ...and sleep.

I remember wanting to throw her out of the room, but my better judgment, a.k.a. general anesthesia, prevented me from doing so.

Reflecting back on that moment now, I realize this had nothing to do with her. My mother loves me unconditionally and only wants the best for me. The entire cause of my frustration at that moment was the story I was telling myself about her not-so-hidden opinion about my choice to have the surgery.

My inability to accept her question as what it was, a simple string of words, and instead making it into a judgment-laden objection that I had to defend against, was the sole source of my anger.

What I was dealing with in that situation, and countless others in my life where I believed the jabs and judgments of others was them "hating" on me or being naysayers, is what I now call *functional schizophrenia.*

Before anyone gets offended and uses this book as a starter log in their fireplace or unleashes a social media campaign against my insensitivity for serious mental health issues, please know that I am in no way making light of actual schizophrenia or those who suffer from it.

This description, not to be confused with a diagnosis, is of my experience and is akin to talking to yourself, but with more dire consequences. It is when we seem to take our inner voices so seriously that we can't see where they end and we begin.

One of the main differences between real schizophrenia and functional schizophrenia is that functional schizophrenia is based on a simple fundamental misunderstanding—like the entire Prisoner perspective—and can be activated or annihilated at any given moment, almost instantly.

I'm not ignoring the fact that, at times, there are people around us who seem to cover the entire spectrum of *generous and unwelcomed teacher*, from those who are passively (or passive-aggressively) unsupportive all the way to those who are committed to helping us see just how stupid, unreasonable, and irrational we are being. But thinking there is a direct cause-and-effect connection between their opinions and our experience of their opinions is our fundamental misunderstanding and, simultaneously, our roadmap to freedom.

In the hospital bed that day, I wasn't hearing the voice of my mother, though it certainly sounded that way. I was hearing the voice of an interpreter, a long-term resident in the beachfront condo of my mind. An over-zealous, loose-lipped grouch of a storyteller, who had, for the majority of my life up to this point, been wildly effective at helping me to create the frustration, upset, hopelessness, and anger I experienced on a daily basis.

When we believe, incorrectly, that our issues stem from someone or something outside of us, the Prisoner voice of our functional schizophrenia has no choice but to go into manipulation-and-management mode. We try to mold and modify the people and situations around us, which as we have all experienced is a complete life-suck and a never-ending waste of our time and energy. Luckily there is a much more effective way—the way of the Self-Leader.

The issue causing our despair and distress is not the event, the person, or the comments they make. The issue is our interpreter. The issue is that we make significant and true what the interpreter

tells us. Their imaginary omnipotence and authority convince us a little too easily.

The funniest part of the whole thing (okay, it didn't seem funny at all when I first realized it but became hilarious shortly thereafter) was that I hired him, I trained him, and I promoted him to higher and higher levels in my company (consciousness). It got to the point that he was running so much of the daily operations that I would defer to him without ever second guessing his interpretations or decisions.

The first step is acknowledging that this interpreter exists—not as a scapegoat to absolve ourselves of responsibility but to start to tease out and separate who we are from what we think.

The next step is gaining an understanding of how to deal with the interpreter so we can experience the transformational effects of Self-Leadership in our everyday lives.

Before we get into the how, though, what if I told you that this debilitating voice, the ringleader of our mental chatter that lives inside of each of us, hiding out in the foxholes of our brains is…a baby—a little brazen bundle of bogusness that is masterful at turning innocent and fleeting thoughts into ticking time bombs.

He sits and waits (sucking his thumb, playing with a stuffed animal or something equally menacing) for orders to wage war on our happiness, from the most opportune position possible…within the sacred borders of our thoughts.

He (or she) is, in my imagination, a *baby assassin*! Don't you just want to cuddle him?

Whenever we think we are upset at someone for the comments they make about us, we are actually triggered from the inside out.

The baby assassin hears the opinions, criticisms, and judgments from others as a blaringly loud siren and a blindingly bright strobe light. They wake him up, launch him out of his crib (I'm imaging him in a little ninja outfit, smoke machine on full blast and him landing in a power pose), and send him into seek-and-destroy mode with our moods and emotions.

As menacing and diabolical as this baby assassin sounds (and hopefully I haven't ruined your love for children), I have found a fairly simple way to shift from being a Prisoner to a Self-Leader when he is throwing a tantrum in my head.

When I feel the emotional hijack starting to surface, I slow down and imagine this fictional little intruder as a real infant—a human being that exists *outside of me*. I envision him lounging in my mind, just a few inches tall, and me carefully pinching the back of the collar of his little ninja onesie between my thumb and index finger, lifting him up and out of my head and gently placing him into an imaginary, but very modern and swanky, bassinet that sits in front of me.

Once I see that the baby exists outside of me, then I also know I can't possibly be the baby. I finally see him for what he is—a harmless, innocent, outspoken creation of my mind who is much easier to be with when I give him his own space and can view him from a safer distance.

This is also where we break the pattern of functional schizophrenia and can recognize that the baby is not the enemy— he simply doesn't know any better. He hasn't learned how to take control of his experience of the world like we have. He just reacts to whatever is going on in the outside world—and he obviously hasn't read this book.

Sometimes when the baby assassin is feeling extra persistent, even when we evict him from our minds and sit him down in front of us, he continues to scream and nag and try to talk us out of what we want to do. He rapid fires excuses like *"You have no idea what you're doing!"* or *"You've never done that before!"* or *"Who are YOU to be doing that?"* What then?

Contrary to much of what you may have seen or read in the personal growth world, I am not going to ask you to fight off, overcome, push through, or do any other clenched-fist activities.

It isn't because I am a tree-hugging pacifist or that my backbone has been weakened because I just watched one of those animal cruelty commercials with Sarah McLachlan. It's because those things simply aren't effective, and they waste more (time, energy, and effort) than they create.

When a real baby cries, do we try to rationalize with the baby? Do we try to talk him out of his sadness or argue or fight with him? Do we punish him? We could, but what typically happens when we object to, fight with, or punish children (or people in general)? They rebel, they hold even more steadfastly, and they are unwavering in their beliefs because they, like most of us, default to protecting themselves at all costs. They feel their power has been taken away, and they act out even more defiantly than they did initially. This is true for adults and children alike.

What is the more loving and effective response that most *enlightened* parents typically default to in service of their young child? What lowers the resistance in others and ourselves when we are stubborn and close-minded? It is an approach of warmth, love *(including self-love)*, acknowledgment, and acceptance *(including self-acceptance)*. Not making the baby wrong for his emotions and simply loving him unconditionally.

When you exhibit Self-Leadership, you can stand strong in your willingness to live in and from a place of love instead of fear. Fear tries to fight away and force out our thoughts and diminishes our ability to be clear and purposeful. Love opens us up to possibilities. It sees that everything we are experiencing is perfect and is ultimately for our greatest good.

You can fall in love with *what is* at any given moment while being playfully devoted to experimenting and having fun with the process, regardless of how often the baby is awoken or put in a bad mood.

You are in charge, and you have the choice of whether or not you allow him to take over the show. Choosing Self-Leadership means you can experience a sense of love, courage, and power that nobody can take away from you, especially not an imaginary baby, because even though you love him, you love you more.

Deep Shame Thrombosis

> *We don't stop playing because we grow old;*
> *we grow old because we stop playing.*
>
> —George Bernard Shaw

How do we get children excited about scary, boring, mundane tasks, or things they just don't want to do, like cleaning their room, eating their veggies, or taking a bath? We simply say, "Let's play a game!"

They perk up and get energized. We think we're manipulating them, but if anything, they're manipulating us. We didn't trick them. They are getting exactly what they want: fun—the thing that, besides sugar, is the biggest motivator for children.

However, somewhere along the way, we *unlearn* that simple truth and decide instead to try on the *adult* way, a much more sophisticated way to get motivated—beating ourselves up!

We try to motivate ourselves with shame and guilt. We believe that some level of self-inflicted abuse and harmful exploitation will

somehow coax out our greatest selves. But if beating ourselves up worked, it would have worked by now, don't you think?

What if we could somehow tap back into what worked so well for us as children? What if fun, even in some highly refined and sophisticated "adult" form, was something we could use to motivate us instead of shame, guilt, and obligation?

What I'm really asking is, if you found a way to stop *must-erbating* and *should-ing* on yourself, get rid of the forcing and fighting, and instead have the process feel more effortless, do you think that would have a positive effect on your success and happiness?

My dear friend, creative partner, and mentor Steve Chandler and I believed in this so deeply that we created our *The Not-So-Serious Life* Internet TV series to explore how much more effective a shameless, light, humorous and playful approach to life and business can be! We get messages all the time from our loyal viewers saying how transformational it has been to hear us simplify and *humorize* their big, daunting problems and how seeing the world through this lens has led them to experiment with living in a more creative and Not-So-Serious way with incredible results.

Bottom line, this isn't just some feel-good fluff to make you smile; this stuff actually works!

In my experience (and by experience, I mean years of Prisoner-based shaming myself into "getting stuff done"), one fun option to start living in a more playful and Not-So-Serious way is to bring some *gamification* into our world.

Gamification may seem like a big fancy millennial word, but it is a very simple alternative to shaming ourselves into action. Essentially, gamification takes elements of the fun and challenge that games

bring into our lives and creatively integrates them into the different tasks, projects, and ideas that we desire to take action on.

It is important to note here that unless you first have raised your level of consciousness to a place where you can be creative, deciding how to *gamify* your way into action may still seem difficult. We don't want the quest for fun ways to gamify your life to be one more thing to shame yourself about if clear ideas on how to do that aren't immediately coming to mind.

The challenge I have seen my clients encounter is that when they try to make a game of something by using the same heavy, annoyed, entitled, or Prisoner-based thinking that had them trying to force themselves to take action in the first place, the fun needle doesn't move.

We are much more effective at creating games around our challenges and opportunities when we first make the choice to shift our energy and approach from that of a Prisoner to a Self-Leader. We will feel almost instant access to the part of us that can make doing the dishes, completing a huge project, or making sales calls into an effortless, and dare I say, enjoyable experience.

In my TEDx Talk entitled "How to Manufacture Fascination and Engineer Enthusiasm," I share a simple and deeply powerful "fascination hack" that can help us make this shift in seconds! You can watch the talk here: http://www.TheJasonGoldberg.com/TEDx

Beyond what I shared in my TEDx Talk, another way we can raise our level of consciousness before starting down the path of gamification is to ask ourselves, or have someone ask us, powerful questions.

These types of questions dive below the surface of what our analytical minds are capable of, point us inward, and activate a part of our brains that we have allowed to take a nap while the bored

and miserable part of us has been onstage accepting an award for Worst Supporting Actor in a drama.

I remember being in a session with a woman we'll call Madeline, a leader in a vacation sales organization who was desperately trying to get her team to improve their sales performance.

She had given them ample training opportunities and tried the buddy-buddy approach, hoping they would improve if she acted like their best friend. She tried the command-and-control route at one point, stopping just short of threats, ultimatums, and tarring and feathering, with consequences to come unless they turned things around.

During one of our sessions, I asked if she would be *game*, no pun intended, to experiment with the idea of gamification to help her with her sales team's performance. I mean, what else could she do besides taking their families hostage or requiring management approval for bathroom breaks?

She was open (it was probably more desperation than true willingness) and so I started by asking her what her favorite board game had been growing up. She quickly said, "Battleship" (and now the command-and-control approach made perfect sense). As we talked more about why she loved it, it was obvious from her nostalgia and excitement that she wished that I had the game there, so she could show me just how good she was at it.

What we discovered in that session was that she had learned the elements of strategy, competition, surprise, winning, patience, analysis, decision making, dealing with pressure, and ethics from playing Battleship.

Oh boy, can you imagine enticing a kid to learn all of those things from a book or through force or bribes? But when you can package

those teachings in a way that engages the innate, competitive, creative, high-spirited nature we were born with, everything changes.

With all of that in her awareness now and with her energy visibly shifting from plagued to playful, I asked her a question that I hoped would get her a little further into the possibility-based thinking of a Self-Leader. "Madeline, if Parker Brothers, the creator of Monopoly, came to you and said, 'If you could make your team's performance challenge into a board game that people would actually play, and we'll give you a million dollars for doing so, what would that game look like?'"

This question shifted her thinking completely. It was no longer about the perils and despair of her team's numbers. Instead, it was a chance to get back to her preteen self and make up how she would want to play that game.

What we came up with was a series of fun components, including a leaderboard, creative recognition, and the ability for top performers to earn rewards they cared about, including being able to submerge her and other managers into a dunk tank with the tagline, "You sunk my leadership." Not surprisingly, people wanted to engage as a team in these games, their morale improved, and along with it, their engagement and performance.

It is a big misconception that work and play cannot coexist—that levity and playfulness have no business in business. Not only can they occupy the same space at the same time but it is even possible to blend them to the point that we can't see where one ends and the other begins.

It brings to mind a quote that an incredible coach and human named Steve Hardison introduced me to. Hardison, known as "The Ultimate Coach" is one of the most passionate and intensely loving

men I have ever met, so I was a more than a little frightened when he decided to take me on a field trip to a local cemetery near his home in Mesa, Arizona. When we arrived, he walked me over to a bench that was placed adjacent to his burial plot, which he had already purchased for himself and his wife Amy, both of whom are still living. On that bench was inscribed this quote by L.P. Jacks:

> A master in the art of living draws no sharp distinction between his work and his play; his labor and his leisure; his mind and his body; his education and his recreation. He hardly knows which is which. He simply pursues his vision of excellence through whatever he is doing, and leaves others to determine whether he is working or playing. To himself, he always appears to be doing both.

That's the beauty of gamification, of tapping back into the default mode of play we chose, without a second thought, when we were children.

This is a powerful trait of Self-Leadership—using our high-spirited, creative minds to blur the line of thinking, motivation, behaviors, and actions, between the things that we believe we have to do and those that we want to do. If Steve Hardison can embrace that separation at his final resting place, I think we all can do it while we have the gift of being on this side of the dirt.

When you step into your power as a Self-Leader, you allow yourself to be pulled by a game instead of being pushed by your shame. As a result, whatever you choose to create will come with far more enjoyment and effortlessness.

The Upside of Comparison

When I was 9 years old, Star Trek came on. I looked at it and I went screaming through the house, "Come here, mom, everybody, come quick, come quick, there's a black lady (Nichelle Nichols, playing the part of lieutenant Uhura on Star Trek) on television and she ain't no maid!" I knew right then and there I could be anything I wanted to be.

—Whoopi Goldberg

What Whoopi Goldberg (no relation) did there is a key way of being and acting that separates the Self-Leader from the Prisoner. When she saw someone else do something extraordinary, she didn't fall into a pit of quicksand that would drown her based on her perceived

limitations. She didn't focus on the imaginary scarcity of her options that would prevent her from doing something like Nichelle had done. She saw the evidence of this stranger's success as a *roadmap* and not a *roadblock.*

Whether or not Whoopi actually wanted to be an actress is irrelevant. That instant insight and realization brought about a breadth of new possibilities that, just moments earlier, she didn't even know existed.

It is just like if you had only eaten chocolate ice cream your entire life, unaware of any other flavors, and a good friend introduced you to strawberry. It doesn't necessarily mean that strawberry ice cream becomes your new go-to flavor, but the mere existence of a new option can help with the development of a brand new *created future,* something a Self-Leader takes pride in actively inventing—as opposed to the *default future* that a Prisoner succumbs to.

New options, even those introduced by others' accomplishments, can help us ask new and novel questions about what else is possible for us.

For example: "What would the two flavors mixed together taste like? How else can I combine chocolate and fruit in a non-frozen dessert? What would the scent of chocolate and strawberries bottled together smell like as an air freshener or perfume?" All of these new ideas to explore and concepts to experiment with were created simply because your friend introduced you to a new ice cream flavor.

This distinction between the way a Prisoner and a Self-Leader interprets the victories and successes of others is key. When we see the accomplishments of others as roadblocks, our Prisoner thinking kicks in. We become deflated and desperate, and we begin to believe

that our own limitations and the "scarcity of the universe" are the nails in the coffin to our success.

When we operate with this lower level of consciousness, and the mental chatter takes over this internal conversation, we start making excuses—namely, for the unfair advantages the successful people have that we don't. And then, to give our Prisoner muscle a high-impact workout, we create a feeling of guilt or shame and punish ourselves (or our parents) for not having those same advantages.

A gentle, creative shift into Self-Leadership, however, has us see those successes as a frame of reference, *a proof of concept*, an expansion of our definition of *doable*, a model of what is possible with the right mix of creativity, belief, action, and patience.

It takes us from the despair and resignation of "There is no way I can do what they did!" to the excitement and wide-grinning enthusiasm of "If they could do that, what else is possible for me!?"

In seeing the path of others as a roadmap instead of a roadblock, it can also be helpful to think of what an actual roadmap illustrates. It shows countless points of origin and seemingly infinite destinations—all available for exploration and experimentation. Just like a physical map, this metaphorical roadmap does not illustrate *the* path, but instead numerous paths. From the map's point of view, there is no preferred or right path for us. That decision is completely ours. We just have to choose.

I must be oversimplifying this though. If we have unlimited access to this powerful device, why aren't more of us where we want to be? One reason may be that some of us are using it incorrectly. It's like trying to write a love letter with the eraser end of the pencil, trying to type on a keyboard that has been turned upside down, or trying to use the brake pedal to accelerate in a vehicle. The

ineffectiveness rests not with the instrument but with the way we have been playing it.

So much of my clients' and my success in personal reinvention and Self-Leadership has come from understanding that the power of the roadmap was not in following the exact path of those who came before us. It was not in looking at their journey and copying their "what," the specific steps they took. Instead, it was in modeling and embodying their, "who," the inner qualities, characteristics, and way of being from which their realities were created.

One of the most impactful things I have ever done for myself is creating a "who do I need to *be*" list. I now have nearly all of my clients do the same exercise. When they say they have goals that involve a certain level of success with money, business, health, or relationships, I don't ask them to create a detailed 5-year plan to make that fantasy into a reality. Instead, we slow down, and I ask them, "Who would you need to *be* for those things to happen?" The *being* must come before the *doing*.

For example, on my own list, there is nothing about how much money I will make, how many talks or trainings I deliver, how many books I sell, how many vacations I take, or how much body fat I have. Instead it has characteristics of my *being* such as relaxed, enthusiastic, restful, unattached to outcomes, courageous and playful. I know that when I embody those qualities, which are always present, though I don't always consciously choose them, it exponentially increases the effectiveness of any tasks, plans, projects, or strategies I decide to execute.

After you finish this chapter, put down this book and spend 15 minutes creating your own list. You will know what belongs on it because you can look at the clues from your own life of when you were at your best—when you were in flow, feeling confident,

competent, and powerful. List those qualities and then put that list somewhere you can see it, review it, and breathe it in every morning. Don't underestimate the simplicity of this exercise. It has the power to change the way you show up in the world and, in turn, what you are able to create.

Spending time with and studying the path of the people I admired as an inspirational and aspirational case study, and understanding the mindset and being that they embody, allowed me to discover those aspects in my own character. It also allowed me to see what beliefs, excuses, or assumptions to challenge and release in order to get there. In my experience, this is what the majority of the "successful people" we look up to have done.

We often see our heroes and champions, the astonishingly talented people who came before us, as trailblazers. Those who practice Self-Leadership know that the power lies not in the specific trail someone blazed, but instead in how those individuals took ownership of their future *(by taking ownership of their present)*, called upon the highest version of themselves, and chose to blaze any trail at all.

There is nothing stopping you from doing the same but you, and that is probably the best news you've heard all day!

Stop Being So Cautious!

I will not let anyone walk through my mind with their dirty feet.

—Mahatma Gandhi

People who "care" about us want to keep us safe. They want to make sure that we *proceed with caution.*

"I hope you know what you're doing; starting a new business in these tough economic times could be a very bad idea."

"I have to warn you; I have a friend who applied at that company and didn't make it past the first interview."

"I hate to be the bearer of bad news, but I know people who started that diet and gave up within two weeks."

"I know she seems nice, but be careful. Don't you remember what happened the last time you opened your heart to someone?"

But what would happen if we focused less on being *cautious* (the heavy and debilitating approach of a Prisoner) and more on being *conscious* (the light, level, and loving focus of a Self-Leader)?

I'm not talking about being reckless, dangerous, or careless—there is little to no real *consciousness* to speak of there.

I mean being aware of moments where you feel stress, doubt, or fear and being mindful of where those emotions originate; from either being *future-focused* or *past-paralyzed*.

I mean noticing when those feelings occur and choosing to slow down into the present moment, where you need nothing more than what you have and where you are perfectly safe and secure.

I mean living in a place where you learn, grow, and flourish by coming from a relaxed and enthusiastic flow-based mindset (where creativity, possibilities, and opportunities are born) instead of being a Prisoner to the fixed mindset that tells you each decision is all or nothing, win or lose, live or die.

I mean being awake to the fact that our response-ability (our ability to respond) is a more effective element to focus on than lengthy analysis, the pursuit of perfection, or trying to remove uncertainty from our journey altogether.

The concept of *consciousness* is no longer reserved for quinoa-farming, new-age hipsters or paramedics reporting vital signs ahead of their arrival to the E.R. It is a choice and practice available to every one of us any time we want to go from a place of fear and anxiety to a place of purpose and calm.

The more conscious you choose to be, the less cautious you have to be. This is the understanding and practice of a Self-Leader.

Proceed with consciousness.

You've Got to Come Original

About the most originality that any writer can hope to achieve honestly is to steal with good judgment.

—Josh Billings

There is an obsession in so many of us that if we aren't 100% original in everything we do, that unless we can make ourselves out to be something or someone both exceptional and unattainable by anyone else, we will never be good enough, wealthy enough, and certainly never happy enough.

There is nothing wrong with wanting to be original, to be driven and motivated to create something that no one has ever seen before.

The intention behind wanting to be unique, however, is what leaves us feeling either empty or empowered.

When the quest for originality and individualism comes from Prisoner energy (and you can always tell because the motivation

comes from ego and the fear of not being enough), we are debilitated by a constant sense of pressure.

We try to force ourselves to do something revolutionary from a weak and distracted place instead of something evolutionary from a relaxed and creative state of mind.

When we are creating from the stance of a Self-Leader, we are focused on what would serve the greatest good, what would activate (or re-active) within us the fun and fire that feeds our soul and creativity, and what would allow us to showcase and experiment with our unique gifts, experiences, and voice. That voice, *your* voice, is the only truly original thing that exists.

When we relax into the uniqueness we possess just by virtue of the journey we have embarked on, then the road to originality is paved with more ease, more authentic self-expression, and more prosperity.

I struggled with this quite a bit at the beginning of my journey as a keynote speaker, professional trainer, life coach, and writer. I also see it in nearly everyone I work with at some point during our time together.

I was entranced, enamored, and fascinated by certain people when I first started on this path. They were mentors, colleagues, friends, and complete strangers, each of whom had great success in their respective careers and had done it in a unique way. It was both exciting and inspiring for me.

Focusing on their journey through the lens of my Prisoner thinking had me suffering and struggling with the question, "How will I ever be as good as them?"

The simple but transformational work I went through to shift from a powerless Prisoner who was terrified of and discouraged

by their accomplishments, to a Self-Leader who would see that the qualities I admired in them were already available to me, was a process that involved time, patience, introspection, creativity, and action.

For the better part of a year, I studied them and mimicked certain parts of how they showed up and who they were.

Then something amazing happened; I woke up one day and realized I had my own style. There was no *aha* moment, a day I could point to where my speaking, writing, coaching, and message were seemingly *born*. It was a gradual process of playfully and diligently showing up, doing the work, rinsing, lathering, and repeating.

It wasn't that I was saying something that no one had ever said; it was just that I was saying it through my experience, interpretation, and understanding of it. I didn't claim that I had the right answer or the best answer, or that I knew what was right for everyone else. I was an expert on one thing—my life!

In other words, nobody can *Jason Goldberg* better than I can *Jason Goldberg*!

I started sharing what I knew to be true for me and invited anyone who was interested to see how what I had done could work for them!

What I have come to see is that what I've experienced, what I say, and how I say it resonate with certain people I meet through online communities or at my events and talks. They tell me that the distinctions and understandings I speak about, teach, and coach around are highly impactful in their lives. And in my mind, one of the biggest reasons this happens is that my story, my personality, my character, my heart, and my voice resonate with them and that

somewhere inside of them, they see themselves—something they have access to as well—in those parts of me.

Being who we are without apologizing for it and sharing our hearts is the way we can be of deep service to the world, to create or empower a tribe, to build deeper relationships. It is the most valuable currency we have in the connection-based economy and times we live in.

Now you may be asking, "How do I find out 'who I am'? And besides, didn't you say earlier that there was nothing permanent or pervasive about our personalities—that we are verbs in constant creation-and-reinvention mode?"

Yes, that's true, and I'm so happy you are paying attention! *Who you are* is not about being someone or something now and forever. It is about being someone who can change based on new insights, new thinking, and new actions from moment to moment. This is how Self-Leaders create (and re-create over and over again) who they are.

It isn't about pinpointing a specific label to attach to. It's about developing awareness in each moment as you creatively experiment and find more of your own voice so that *who you are* is always growing, always evolving, always experiencing new influences and inspirations and, like the opening act for the Rolling Stones, is subject to change without notice!

Sticking with the music theme for a minute, in his book *Raise Your Voice*, vocal coach Jaime Vendera writes:

The best way to develop style is by singing along with other singers. ... Choose the singers that inspire you. ... Work on perfecting the part of their technique that you admire ... You want to emulate a singer's taste, not his or her exact sound.

He goes on to say:

> I used to love to sing songs by the 80's rock group Journey, but as hard as I tried, I couldn't sound anything like Steve Perry. ... I finally found my niche the first time I sang "Immigrant Song" by Led Zeppelin. Finally, everything seemed to fit and vocally flow. For me, stylistically, that's who I am. ... [T]hat was the first rock song that gave me freedom and allowed my voice to open up. ... You'll know when you find a song that fits you because it will physically and mentally feel right. Keep singing and you'll eventually find your niche.

You can replace *niche* here with gifts, voice, style, inner genius, magic, whatever elements of yourself that you desire to create or uncover.

The emergence of the most powerful, successful, happy, high-spirited version of you occurs through doing the work and experimenting with the options and possibilities until you feel the physical, mental, and energetic alignment that Jaime talked about. Remember, even the Beatles started as a cover band. Why should your journey be any different (or less fun)?

With the confidence that eventually came from doing the work (notice that my confidence was a "result of," not a "prerequisite for" doing the work), I followed my enthusiasm, developed my voice, and finally started to swap what I thought I should be doing with what energized the best parts of me.

Then and only then was I finally able to answer my original, heavy, anxious question of "How will I ever be as good as them?"

The answer: I never would! Because they are them, and I am me. And me being me is the only thing 100% original in the world.

As Austin Kleon, one of those people I used to be terrified of and discouraged by and who I now love and find inspiration from, once said, "You don't want to look like your heroes, you want to see like your heroes."

By seeing the world through the eyes of your heroes and standing on the shoulders of the giants who came before you, there are no limits to what you can create and no doubt that it will end up being uniquely you.

As Dr. Seuss said, "Today you are You, that is truer than true. There is no one alive who is Youer than You."

Creative Codependence

You develop a team to achieve what one person cannot accomplish alone. All of us alone are weaker, by far, than if all of us are together.

—Mike Krzyzewski,
coach of the 1992 US Olympic Basketball Dream Team

Usually, when people talk about codependency, it is viewed as a "bad thing." For example, in romantic relationships, it means that you rely on your partner in unhealthy ways to meet your own emotional needs.

When using the creativity that comes along with being a Self-Leader, however, you can create a form of codependence that serves you! *Creative Codependence*, as I now call it, is like a form of teamwork that occurs when you become codependent on…yourself!

If you're confused and wondering if I either stopped taking or need to up the dosage on my meds, let me explain what I mean.

I am talking about reaching out to, leaning on, and calling upon the version of you that can handle whatever the situation at hand calls for. I get that this may be starting to sound like a milder form of multiple personalities, and I'm perfectly okay with that. I know it works because it isn't a coping mechanism but an approach that primes us for powerful, purposeful creation.

When we believe that the characteristics or qualities we need in order to be a powerful leader, a fully present spouse, a fearless sales person, or an unconditionally loving parent are beyond our abilities or are only reserved for certain "special" people, we begin to act as Prisoners to our perceived shortcomings. We become hopeless and helpless. Not only does this outside-in, unproductive story not serve us, it simply isn't true.

When I am giving a talk to a corporate audience or delivering a keynote at a convention, and I share this concept, I get a wide variety of reactions from the crowd. The most popular of those reactions is something I don't have a name for yet. But it resembles whatever the facial expression equivalent of "Yeah right, Mr. Self-Leadership—now tell me how I can manifest a Rolls-Royce and a mansion in Bora Bora with vision boards and meditation" would be.

The truth is, I have no idea how to do any of that because Creative Codependence isn't about a specific result or outcome. Instead, it's about who you are (or can be) given the situation or circumstance in front of you.

It isn't something you do in order to get something else. It isn't about becoming the person you were "meant" to be—whatever that even means. And it isn't about faking it until you make it.

It is simply an invitation to notice that no matter who you are, what thoughts you think, what actions you take, or what perspective

you have on the world, at this very moment, there are multiple somebodies inside of you, with limitless abilities, aptitudes, and attitudes, waiting to be called upon.

These are the internal experts and heroes you've been looking for to save you or help unravel what seems like an unsolvable problem, to support you in an insurmountable challenge, or to lead the dialog in a difficult conversation. They are available to you regardless of whether you are in a place of calm or crisis — though they are much easier to access in a calm, peaceful, and mindful state.

If you are still aren't sold on this Creative Codependence stuff (and I don't want you to be "sold"; I just want you to be willing to test these off-the-wall rants of a madman for yourself), let me share a quick scenario with you. Then you can decide for yourself if it has any merit.

Let's say you have a young son. You're standing next to him on a sidewalk next to a busy street and all of a sudden, he darts off after a bouncy ball that has slipped from his hands. In a flash, he runs into traffic and right into the path of a speeding car. If someone doesn't intervene, he is certain to be killed.

Now, if Creative Codependence and all of these various versions of you I have mentioned didn't exist, then you would see what was happening and not do anything about it. And that would make complete and total sense given who you may say you are in less dire circumstances.

You would say that you're not normally a very brave person. You're not someone who takes risks. You aren't the type to do things without thinking them through and making sure that you are selecting the best and safest option.

But what ends up happening instead? Something seemingly miraculous occurs. At that moment, the version of you that is fully equipped to break out of the prison that restricts you to what you would *normally* do instantly emerges and, inexplicably, you do what needs to be done in that situation.

This might look like you running after your son, grabbing his arm, and launching him and yourself back to safety like a heroic comic book character! Good thing you were so Creatively Codependent!

This is proof that at any moment, not just in situations where life and limb are at risk, we have access to these different versions of ourselves. To me, their existence is no longer in question. The only question is whether we step into our power of Self-Leadership and choose to embody them or we default back to the Prisoner excuses that have convinced us for too long that *who we are* is static and fixed.

Let me introduce you to a powerful visualization technique that you can use to practice this Creative Codependence. Imagine that your consciousness is housing the metaphysical equivalent of a championship sports team, like the USA Basketball Dream Team from the 1992 Olympics (I feel comfortable putting this reference in because I know next to nothing about sports, and even I know about the Dream Team!).

This team of all-stars was the best the NBA had to offer, and each player played a pivotal role in the team's astonishing success at the Olympic games. Some were defensive powerhouses, others were three-point sharpshooters, and still others were experts at finding the smallest possible gap in the traffic of the opponent's team to feed the ball into a player in the post for a quick score.

What I have found over the years of working on myself and with my clients is that we have the same Dream Team available to us at all times.

Now close your eyes and visualize that 10, 20, 50, 100 "players" are surrounding you right now, standing in a half circle 10 feet in front of you.

The players look just like you, and they have huge smiles on their faces. You can feel that they have your back, they want you to succeed, and they are ready to serve you in any way they can at a moment's notice.

Instead of their names being sewn on their jerseys, qualities you want access to are printed across them. There is No. 24 "Courageous," No. 16 "Compassionate," No. 7 "Calm," and good old No. 49 "Creative." Every possible feeling, emotion, skill, characteristic, quality, or power you need to excel in the game of life is right there in front of you, at your disposal, under your control. This is your team!

Each of the team members is waving their hands at you, eager and enthusiastic, clamoring and shouting, "Coach, put me in. I can make this happen. I know I can do this. Let me help!" So why not give them a chance? Choose them, lean on them, allow them to embody your being, and then approach whatever you are faced with from that place—fired up and ready to go!

Self-Leadership is recognizing that inside of you—a single player—is the entire team. Inside of this one shell is any and every type of person you need to help you create, handle, and fulfill anything you truly want in your life.

The "21-Day Habit" Myth

> *We are what we repeatedly do. Excellence, then, is not an act, but a habit.*
>
> —Aristotle

We've probably all heard about the rule of 21 days (or some other arbitrary number) that says you must do something for 21 days straight for it to become a habit, an effortless part of your routine.

But what had always challenged me was that I rarely made it to 21 days. And any time I had a 3- or 7- or 18-day backslide, I would beat myself up like I owed me money!

Waiting three full weeks to feel like you've made a positive change and hoping that it happens on autopilot from then on may work well for a lot of people. But I was way too impatient for that.

Self-Leaders, those who are truly response-able, understand that a more effective way to get results and create habits is far simpler. For them, it isn't about creating a habit now that has to be done

every day for the rest of their lives. It's about creating a habit that they will commit to doing just for today, or JFT for short.

My clients are very familiar with this acronym because of how often I use it. At times, it is all I need to say to snap them out of their Prisoner-mode of goal-fixation and achievement-obsession and into their natural state of Self-Leader—focusing on consistency over intensity.

This is not just some anecdotal motivation to get you off the hook from long-term commitment or to overly simplify challenging work. This was the core of my practice, back in 2011, when I started on my weight loss journey and eventually lost 130 pounds.

My weight loss voyage (not just in losing physical weight but all of the types of weight and heaviness—mental, emotional, financial, etc.—that I carried around as a Prisoner) is now a key part of the message I share when speaking and training at conferences and for corporations.

After I share my story, I often field questions from the audience such as: "How did you lose 130 pounds? Tell me how you did it." "How did you get the weight off?" "How did you keep the weight off?"

At first when they would ask me those questions, I'd go into logistics. I'd tell them about my weight loss surgery and how I had to change my relationship with food and have a consistent fitness practice—all the things that Google could answer far better and with more detail and structure than I ever could off-the-cuff.

But after a while, I finally realized that was not the whole story, and it wasn't how I actually had lost the weight. In fact, I hadn't lost 130 pounds. I had lost 1 pound, but I had done it 130 times. This is the power of JFT in all of its consistent, impactful glory.

When we try to create a habit and then label ourselves failures if we fall even slightly off track, we become Prisoners, preoccupied by a need for *perfection* on something that was only ever meant to be a *practice*. We waste our energy, our power, and our creativity and allow ourselves to be sabotaged by something that we created in the first place. Once again, we are both the captives and the captors, behind the bars and simultaneously the holders of the key.

In Malcolm Gladwell's book *Outliers*, he talks about the 10,000-hour rule. Essentially, the rule states that you need 10,000 hours of practice in any particular discipline to be a master of that domain. I believe success and results come from doing *the work* consistently and agree with Gladwell and people like George Leonard, who talk about living your life on a continuous path of mastery.

But what inevitably happens with so many of the people I have worked with (and again, "people I have worked with" always includes myself) is that we see that unfathomable number, and immediately it becomes daunting. We calculate that 10,000 hours is going to take us X number of years, and we don't want to commit to that or don't know if we can commit to that. And the inner chatter goes, if we are going to fail eventually, why even start?

But what is failure anyway? It is a very ambiguous concept, and when I quiz my clients about it, more often than not, they don't even have a picture of what it would look like—besides "bad" of course.

We're letting something we don't even have a definition of rule our lives and lead our decisions.

Though failure may not be clear to articulate, this is what it may look like: We commit to some big, lofty, impossible goal, and once we miss the mark by even the slightest amount, we start to focus on

how non-habitual we have been in the past and how this is evidence that we can't possibly be disciplined.

We treat a momentary break in our practice as irrefutable proof that trying at all is a waste of time and energy. That keeps us in the past and makes us spend more time and more of our precious energy being prisoners of being Prisoners—*beating ourselves up* for the past instead of *building ourselves up* for the future.

That's why it is so important for us to see these habits as rituals or routines that we are only required to do today, JFT, without projecting that into the story of the future. Remember, these are commitments, not commandments—not nearly as serious or significant as we tend to make them.

In much the same way my journey of weight loss took place one single pound (and one stressful thought) at a time, the key to getting 10,000 hours of practice—or creating a new habit or routine—is to get just one hour of practice one day, and then, the next day to get one more hour and one more hour and one more hour.

As Dusan Djukich says in his book, *Straight-Line Leadership*, powerfully and succinctly, "Stop stopping."

The great thing about "stopping stopping" is that it is not based on a feeling. Whether or not to do something just for today is never an emotional decision. It's strictly a matter of choosing.

Once you make the vow to be dedicated, even just for today, that dedication is as unaffected by your fleeting emotional states as a forest fire is when you blow on it.

Just for today is your new best friend, your new benchmark for success, your new basis for celebration. *Just for today* is the way a Self-Leader turns incremental change into massive transformation.

Not Every Shot Is the Game-Winning Shot

The only time you mustn't fail is the last time you try.

—Charles Kettering

I remember being contacted by a person who was considering hiring me to speak at his upcoming convention. Someone who had seen me speak at another event referred him to me and vouched for my abilities, so he already had some idea of what I do.

This was a pretty big opportunity for me, and I noticed that about 30 minutes before the scheduled call, some nervousness and anxious energy started creeping in.

I immediately started playing out in my head how I could make myself look and sound impressive so he would book me. How could I show him, in this first conversation, that I was the perfect person for the gig? How could I let him know everything he needed

to know about me to make the decision right there on the spot and hire me?

This wasn't the energy I wanted to bring to the call, so I decided to quiet my mind (and my ego) a bit by meditating for 20 minutes.

I cannot overstate how centering, soothing, and creativity-sparking it can be to sit in silence or take a walk outside. You don't have to know how to meditate; you only have to know how to sit and close your eyes or walk (or crawl or roll or mosey) and allow yourself to do so with no other responsibilities or demands in sight. With some practice, it will become easy for you to grab the metaphorical popcorn and watch the movie of your mind, without the need to reach out, interact with, or attach to your thoughts.

Trust me, do this every day (or at least just for today), and you will experience what Richard Carlson and Joseph Bailey have called "slowing down to the speed of life." It is one of the most impactful practices I employ in my life, and it is responsible for much of my transformation into Self-Leadership on a moment-by-moment basis.

When I was done with my meditation, something powerful occurred to me: Though this upcoming telephone conversation was a shot at building a relationship with this person and having him decide whether or not to hire me, it was not the only shot I would ever have.

I had believed, incorrectly and ineffectively, that the only way to be "successful" was to build a thriving, flourishing, deep connection and relationship in that one phone call. This was not to say that couldn't happen, but my belief had been that if I didn't make it happen on this call, it would never happen. I would be forgotten, written off, or rejected.

Now here is the gift in this and any other heavy, debilitating, and disserving belief: Whether the belief is true or not is irrelevant; it only matters if I give it any significance and how I show up when I do so.

If I had remained a Prisoner to that belief and let it guide my thoughts, feelings, and behaviors, how do you think it would have affected the way I would have showed up to that call? Would I have showed up relaxed? Genuinely interested and curious? Energized and optimistic? Ready to serve?

Doubtful.

What is more likely is that I would have showed up desperate. Overeager. Needy. Maybe even manipulative and certainly trying to "win friends and influence people." Projecting some level of gravitas and worthiness instead of allowing the conversation to be about two people simply connecting, without an agenda, posturing, or any expectations.

I was once interviewed on a podcast about entrepreneurship, and I remember the host enthusiastically saying, "So JG, one thing we always do on this show is ask our guests to give us their best elevator pitch! You have 15 seconds to give us the goods and have us wanting more! GO!"

For a split second, I thought about going for it, even though I had nothing prepared. But instead I stopped, took a deep breath, and said, "I don't have an elevator pitch. Why would I ever try to rush a relationship and skip the natural progression of a human connection in 15 seconds? If I had 15 seconds with someone, my 'elevator pitch' would be, 'Hi, I'm Jason, what's new and exciting in your world?' Any desperate attempt at proving my worth and convincing a stranger to like me instead of slowing down and

viewing our connection as, potentially, the first of many to come would be doing a disservice to both of us. I like to ask myself, 'If I knew I would see this person for 5 minutes every week for the next year, how would I approach this conversation?'"

The host thanked me for my unconventional perspective. I was never invited back on his show.

A scarcity mentality (which is saturated in ego) has me believe that this is my only shot to "make a good impression." When I release that mentality and instead focus on how I can "make a difference" (which comes from a place of service), I can *be* on the call or in a meeting or at a networking event or on a first date without an attachment to the outcome.

This highly relaxed and untethered way of being allowed my prospective client and me to really connect. He shared his story and what was important to him, and he was able to get a sense of me. And I, instead of trying to manage his impression of me, was able to be present during our time together with no expectation of how it needed to play out or what would happen at the end of the call.

How would you show up differently if you went on your next sales call, first date, or job interview without the thought that you had been handed the ball to take the game-winning shot—that it was all or nothing, and you had to shoulder the responsibility and pressure to make that happen? How would that free you up to be a true Self-Leader, a powerful creator, and a conduit for the best version of you to show up?

The next time someone hands you the ball in one of these situations, how can you pretend that you are an enthusiastic

child simply playing a game of H.O.R.S.E. with some of your closest friends?

If you can tap into that level of fun and ease, you will know that even if you "miss," you can jump right back in, laugh it off, chase the ball down, come up with a new and even more creative variation of your shot, and try again. And know that as long as you are willing to keep playing, the game never has to end.

Self-Leaders know that relaxation and creativity are the keys to successful relationships and that those attributes are much more easily accessible when we drop the desperation and expectations.

You Don't Need to Teach Anyone a Lesson

> *Thinking determines life. It is a common habit to blame life upon the environment. Environment modifies life but does not govern life. The soul is stronger than its surroundings.*
>
> —William James

One afternoon, I was in my *mobile executive office,* a.k.a. inside my car, parked in the lot of a gas station taking a phone call. I parked two spaces over from the coin-operated air machine that people use to fill up their tires, and I pointed my car in the direction of a lovely row of trees to enjoy the inspiring landscape as I spoke to a friend.

Then completely unexpectedly, and undoubtedly when I was about to say something profoundly insightful, my car shook violently! Someone had pulled in fast and furious style, nearly diagonally, to the spaces between my car and the air machine and

smashed the passenger side of my car not once, but twice with the driver side door of his bright red Mustang as he swung it open and exited his vehicle.

I froze and asked my friend to hold on for a minute. In shock and disbelief, I looked over at this idiot. He seemed completely oblivious to the fact that he had just judo chopped my car with his. He was just pumping quarters into the machine and beginning to fill his tires with air.

The rage and feeling of being disrespected started to bubble up inside of me, so I asked my friend if I could call him back, got out of my car, and walked around to the passenger side to assess the damage. I approached the man who was now kneeling down next to his back driver's side tire and sternly said, "Do you know you just hit my car with your door?" as I pointed to the obvious scuff mark with a generous sampling of the signature "Mustang Red" that had clearly come from his door.

To my utter surprise and disbelief, he denied having done it. In one breath, he said he didn't know what I was talking about and in the next, he said I shouldn't have parked so closely to the air machine. He took zero personal responsibility, was careless and apathetic, and was doing anything he could to not incriminate himself or be held accountable for what he had done.

The damage wasn't severe; it was nothing that a good wash and wax couldn't fix. But still, something inside of me in that moment couldn't let it go. I needed him to understand just how rude and insolent he had been and to atone for his wickedness. The cars didn't seem to have a problem with what had happened, but I certainly did!

My work in choosing to be a Self-Leader and learning not to react from an emotionally hijacked state almost fell to the wayside, as I immediately believed that I had to teach him a lesson. I thought I had to get him to care and somehow make him take ownership (which is as backasswords as trying to *teach* someone self-discipline) of what he had just done by schooling him in the way responsible adults are *supposed to* act.

In that moment, I saw that I was getting caught up in my thinking about what should or shouldn't happen next. I took a breath and was able to hit the pause button. Before a single derogatory word reached my lips or my diaphragm expanded to prepare for the wrath that I was mentally prepared to unleash upon him, I slowed down and was able to see how I was creating this experience and, more importantly, that I didn't need to be a Prisoner to it.

What emerged in that moment was an important understanding, an insight that I will never forget...

I didn't need to teach him anything.

That was not what personal responsibility looked like. That was what I did when I was a Prisoner of circumstance, back when it was more important for me to *be* right than to *do* right.

I released making him the villain in the situation — the adversary I needed to hurt and disrespect in a way that was at least equal to how much he had hurt and disrespected me. Even the hurt and disrespect I felt was not caused by him but created by me. No one is capable of hurting or disrespecting me because they don't have direct access to my emotions unless I give them a security badge and walk them into the restricted area.

When I stopped trying to put us on different sides of right and wrong, it didn't let him off the hook; it let me off the hook.

"Hook" seemed an appropriate word choice because had I reacted from a Prisoner mindset, I would have been like a defenseless fish; suffocating and being tossed about, unable to do anything but wait to be released or to die. It is a feeling I was far too familiar with for the first 30 years of my life.

I'm not saying that we can't or shouldn't assert ourselves and ask for, or even insist on getting, what we want or need. Had the damage been greater, I would have calmly asked for his insurance information, and if he had refused, I would have been fine getting the authorities involved. In either scenario, it wouldn't have been about the actions I took, but instead, the person I was *being* when taking those actions. The more calm and conscious we can remain in challenging situations, the more creative we can be about dealing with the issue at hand without having to drop into an unhealthy state of stress, anger, or fear to do so.

By recapturing my innate Self-Leadership, I released the need to change him, to get him to see the light, to have him respond the way I thought he should or the way I would have (or believe I would have) had the shoe been on the other foot. Instead, I allowed the most powerful and relaxed part of me to choose a response that was for my greatest good in that moment. A part of me that led with compassion and understanding, for myself and for him.

Making decisions like those as often as possible is where true freedom and happiness reside. They are chosen and cultivated from the inside out and are unaffected by the actions of others.

If you have a desire to teach others, always start by teaching yourself—pointing your education inward has the most profound and noticeable effect on how you experience the world around you each and every day.

Intentional Drowning

*Clear thinking requires courage
rather than intelligence.*

—Thomas Szasz

I read a statistic that said every day 10 people die from unintentional drowning. I had the interest but not the stomach to try to find the stats on "intentional drowning" and figured such a study probably didn't exist anyway. Because those who succeeded wouldn't be around to tell us whether or not they meant for that outcome or were simply practicing to be Navy Seals or break a Guinness World Record and failed miserably.

But even without any science to back up my curiosity, it still got me thinking.

No matter your position on water, I'll bet you know the sensation of *drowning*. If you are anything like me, you have used that word or its equally overburdened cousins like *swamped, overwhelmed,*

bogged down, or even *really, really busy* to describe your work and life load!

When we describe our situation with this type of language, we are Prisoners of the universe's enormous and powerful metaphorical hand pushing down on our heads, drowning us in a sea of overwork, overburden, and overcommitment which leaves us feeling overfatigued, overtaxed, and just plain over it!

When people come to me for coaching around these challenges, they are almost always looking for time-management tools and techniques. "If only I could figure out how to invent more time or invent more me so that I could get it all done" is where they focus their attention instead of the real opportunity to develop a greater sense of courage and Self-Leadership.

Intentionally *drowning* ourselves comes from what seems to be a good place. We have an intrinsic need to perform, to achieve, to not let people down, and to be liked. So when we choose to be Prisoners to other people's demands, their crises, their urgent needs and wants, it is as if we go underwater for longer and longer periods of time hoping that, at some point, it will finally be enough. That *we* will finally be enough—that we will have proven ourselves and become "made (wo)men" who are permitted to victoriously splash up through the surface of the water, to relax, to be left alone and to breathe clean, fresh, comfortable air for the rest of our days.

As you've probably seen, though, that never seems to happen. I know this to be true as a reformed angry, depressed, morbidly obese people-pleaser who always believed I was just one fire-engulfed chainsaw juggling act away from experiencing ease, flow, and freedom—just one more email, one more promotion, one more favor, one more sacrifice, one more justification.

There is an adage that says, "The sensation of drowning reminds you of everything you ever knew about swimming." If you were literally drowning in some body of water, you would know right away what you needed to do to save your life. Because if you didn't, you would face certain death.

The drowning I'm talking about here isn't much different; it just has an extended timeline. Drowning in our beliefs, our fears, our doubts, and our work is a slower, longer game of death. It's not a matter of minutes but a matter of years—a faint blip on the radar so far off in the distance that we don't believe it can cause any real damage in the long run.

Even less destructive, we may think, is the language we use. Saying we are *swamped* is just an innocent way to talk about feeling frustrated or annoyed by all that we have on our plates, right? Semantics.

But it's like a creaking fan that always bugs us and never really runs smoothly but that we disregard because there are much bigger fires to attend to. We rationalize that it is just an irritating noise that we can choose to ignore because it won't have any real effect on our lives.

Until...the fan stops...in the heat of summer...in the Arizona desert...where it's 120 degrees... and *now* it's a problem.

The fact is that even if you aren't drowning right now but instead are treading water, just one urgent request away from being pulled under, you can't tread water forever. And why would you want to?

Imagine being face-to-face with a king cobra snake. He slithers at an alarming rate, coming right for you. But just as he lunges at you to rip into your neck flesh with his fangs and deposit his

neurotoxins, you grab him by the neck and hold him at bay. Nice work! What a hero! So brave!

But now what?!?

Unless a generous genie happens to walk by and magically transforms him into a cuddly iguana, or you can lull the snake to sleep with a soothing rendition of "Hush, Little Baby," you are a Prisoner to him for the rest of your (or his) life!

The first step in choosing Self-Leadership in the face of drowning involves the (not always easy to face) truth of where the motivation for living this way comes from. That is the reality that was so hard for me to face and that I fought against and tried to convince myself, my coach, and anyone else around me that I was an exception to for so long.

As the director of operations for a tech firm for the better part of a decade, I would regularly send and receive 300+ emails in a day and deal with constant deadlines, "drop everything and do this now" emergencies multiple times per day, and working 70+ hours a week. I believed that I had to do what everyone wanted when they wanted it because it was important and I was important. They (clients, coworkers, bosses, direct reports) needed me, and who was I to deny them access to my greatness?

Even though we did nothing at that company that prevented or presented a danger to the human race, my thought was that they would surely lose life and limb if I didn't put my needs, wants, and focus secondary to theirs. Plus, I had to ignore my health, my relationships, and my well-being because unless I used every second to manage perceptions and prove my worth, how would they continue to see just how important and irreplaceable I was?

But the truth was that always being connected, living at the mercy of my smartphone email ding, and not giving myself the time

I deserved to rest, recharge, and rejuvenate wasn't about me actually *being* important. It was more about me needing to *feel* important — and validated, honored, and accepted. I lived firmly in the belief that my self-esteem, self-importance, and self-worth were directly tied to how much of a savior and martyr I was, sacrificing myself for the "greater good" — something that I would ultimately discover was my weak, fearful, and frail ego.

After years of living in this way and searching high and low for ways to do more with less, thinking that more automation, more systems, and more processes would save me from my self-sacrifice, I finally had an insight that changed everything. The insight was not about what I was doing, but about who I was being. The Prisoner in me thought that the opposite of swamped was delegation or efficiency. The Self-Leader I chose to step into, however, saw that the opposite of swamped, overwhelmed and drowning was simply *courage*.

It isn't that efficiency-based techniques such as time blocking, list making, and the *Pomodoro Technique* are not useful. It's just that doing those things without becoming more of a Self-Leader in your mindset about time will have limited benefit in your results and will just reinforce your Prisoner status. They become one more mechanism to feed the machine of validation, people pleasing, and approval-seeking. You, not your tools, are responsible for setting yourself free.

Being a Self-Leader and bringing courage to a situation where you are drowning means you make decisions about where you focus your time and attention without thinking about how you will be seen by others, whether or not they will approve, or if it pleases them or endears them to you. You consciously choose to look at what you have given your word to complete. Then you recommit

to it, release from it, or renegotiate what it looks like—with yourself and/or whoever else is involved in that agreement.

Courage is not about going back on your word, being flaky or undependable. It is giving yourself the permission to take full ownership of your power, energy, and free will and choosing to slow down into a relaxed, purposeful place before, during, and after making decisions about where you will direct your time and devotion.

It is what allows you to fully focus on the person, relationship, or task in front of you. It is living in a way where you don't fear missing out on something and you don't take seriously the nagging voice that tries to convince you to split yourself up, dilute your attention, and be in a constant state of *faux-ductivity* (that's busyness, distracted thinking, and false promises masking as "productivity").

Courage is both the prerequisite and the result of being clear on the one thing that is a priority and that you can complete right now. Part of what got us into this mess was pluralizing the word *priority* to begin with. There can't be multiple *the* "most important thing," and we take liberties like these with our language to our own detriment.

People will always ask for things from us. They will always have a crisis (or seven). They will always try to tempt us to put aside our better judgment and courage in order to satisfy our intrinsic need to be liked and seen as worthy. They won't change; only *we* have the potential to *be* different.

We can choose to see the freedom in being a Self-Leader. We can be courageous and know that honoring a singularity of purpose and a healthy state of mind is how we can best serve ourselves and the projects and people around us that we commit to.

Let's Go to the Replay!

Don't dwell on what went wrong.
Instead, focus on what to do next.
Spend your energies on moving forward.

—Denis Waitley

For a decade and a half in my various corporate information technology positions, we had this interesting practice called post-mortems. While it sounds like a messy exercise reserved for a medical examiner, in the I.T. world, post-mortems were supposed to be a chance for us to get together and talk about a project after we had finished it. It was an opportunity to discuss what had gone well; what we could have done differently, more efficiently, or more effectively; what we learned; and how we could implement those lessons moving forward.

What it ended up being in reality was a chance to vent and mercilessly blame other members of the team—and often the clients—

for those failings. It was like playing a game of verbal dodgeball where big red faces of blame replaced the big red spheres of pain.

The person most likely to be hit wasn't the nerd, the fat kid or the slow kid (of which I was all three in school). Instead, it was the timid, passive person who would take the blame to keep the peace. Or even worse, there were the people who you would fire your blame at preemptively since you knew that they were going to throw you under the bus the first chance they got! That way, whatever they said was just retaliation and thus would seem less valid.

In the midst of the chaos, confusion, and cutthroat nature of these meetings, I still saw how they could be very valuable if only we approached them from a different energy with a more effective intention.

In a major upgrade to the *post-mortem*, I now do something with my clients and myself called *instant replay*.

After my clients have had a "failed" sales call, or a successful one, or a difficult conversation where they reacted instead of responded, or when they showed up as powerful Self-Leaders instead of defaulting to their previously conditioned, old school Prisoner ways, we look back to debrief on and decode what occurred. We see what was particularly successful or where a higher probability of success could be possible with just a simple tweak of a dial or two.

We don't dwell on the past. We don't look for ways to blame ourselves or others. Instead, we take personal responsibility for things that didn't go the way that we wanted them to, what role we played in that outcome, and what we may do differently in the future—from a place of creativity and possibilities, not shame and blame.

As Self-Leaders, the most effective and often overlooked time to run instant replay is when things go well. When things go

according to plan, we may think that it was just a given or lucky or serendipitous—nothing to learn from that. But in actuality, looking back on that success via *instant replay* can often reveal clues that are portable and transferable to other things we want to be successful in.

I remember coaching a woman we'll call Rhonda. She was a consultant and was building her practice.

At one point, she was trying to enroll people in a powerful seminar she had created. Part of our coaching was to help her fill every seat in the room with people whose lives she would change if they attended.

She had gotten a bit discouraged because while she had a few people sign up initially, she didn't have nearly as many people as she wanted.

When I asked if she was open to run the *instant replay*, she was excited to play but immediately went into what she did "wrong."

I stopped her and said, "Let's slow this down and take a look at what went right. Not just what went right in your tactics and strategies, but how you showed up—your energy, your dedication, your sincerity, your desire to serve—in the conversations with people who signed up that may have contributed to the outcome you created."

Through our conversation, we realized that Rhonda was more effective when she had conversations with people face-to-face than over email. We also discovered that when she chose to embody confidence, and she brought excitement about her workshop to the people she was speaking to (as opposed to other times when she had become discouraged, lost some of her enthusiasm, and became more self-conscious and needy), she had better results in terms of their desire to attend.

Rhonda saw that when she was mindful of being timely and thorough in her follow-up with people who had expressed interest, she had more success than when she allowed herself to get too busy with distractions and ultimately let these people fall to the wayside.

She also realized that when she gave herself ample time to reach out to her potential clients and didn't rush to get them to sign up at the last minute, they would be more excited about joining. When she was relaxed, it created the space for her potential clients to be relaxed as well. There was no sense of desperation, anxiety, or stress, and that also made a huge difference.

When Rhonda and I purposefully and creatively reviewed the *instant reply* in this way, we saw the parts of what she was already doing that was helping to experience success. Then it was as simple as focusing on doing more of those things as opposed to forcibly alleviating all of her perceived shortcomings.

The goal of *instant replay* is not only to celebrate your victories (though that is a fun byproduct) but also to turn what made you successful into a system, so you know what to do more of. Systems give you the measurable and manageable insights and results that show you what to focus on consistently that will likely create a similar outcome.

This isn't about industry best practices or what the experts tell you that you should do. Only you can create the system that is best for you based on your gifts, your experience, your superpowers, and your genius zone.

The system you develop as a result of your *instant replay* will consist of repeatable ways of being, actions, thoughts, and behaviors that light you up so you can show up in a way where results are just a natural outcome of your practice of Self-Leadership.

Systems are also not set in stone; they are living, breathing, and dynamic roadmaps—just like the humans who created them. That is why it is important to note that the results that you are getting are perfect for the system you are using.

Prisoners see a system that is now, or becomes, less-than-effective as a failure, as a sign to give up, or as a reason to make up excuses to not take personal responsibility.

But for the Self-Leaders, if there are parts of their current system that aren't working (anymore), they quickly see the opportunity to run *instant replay* again and get creative to build a new system to test. In the end, successes and failures are just data points; there is nothing inherently good or bad about the results.

Running *instant replay* helps you to focus on what you've done well and to use that honest reflection as the input to build a powerful system that helps you to create the results you want in your life— one play at a time.

Go Ahead and Quit

I'm always thinking about creating.
My future starts when I wake up
every morning... Every day I find something
creative to do with my life.

—Miles Davis

This may not be considered traditional productive thinking, but quitting is a very viable option for all of us. Plenty of people quit, all the time. And they have every logical reason to do so.

Some are fed up with their current circumstances (boss, job, housing, relationship, etc.). Others may want to leave while they are at the top of their game. And some feel like the universe is telling them it's time to move on. These are all seemingly acceptable reasons for throwing in the towel.

So go ahead and quit your job, relationship, ventures, partnerships, school, or anything else you want out of (I have quit at least one of each of those in my lifetime).

But first, ask yourself one question: Are you quitting to avoid something, or are you quitting to *create* something?

In my experience, when I quit to avoid, I am coming from a Prisoner mindset. When I quit to create, however, I am choosing Self-Leadership. I am choosing to redirect my powerful and precious time, energy, and attention to something more meaningful, often something bigger than just me and with a focus that most aligns with and taps into my greatest gifts, my genius zone, and my enthusiasm—from the Greek word *entheos* meaning the "God within."

When we quit to avoid, we are fed up, blaming the world outside of us and operating as Prisoners to the circumstances around us instead of owning our spirit and our choices.

When we leave at the pinnacle of our practice, we may be trying to preserve our past prosperity while protecting ourselves from future failures.

The thing is, when we abdicate personal responsibility and give the universe full reign to make our decisions for us, we are avoiding the potential for some valuable and transformative "face time" with our deepest fears and our biggest dreams. And no matter where we go and what we do, *we* are always the common denominator. So if we quit to escape or avoid and don't address the real opportunity for growth and Self-Leadership, the new thing we choose to do rarely sticks, and the Prisoner perspective slowly, or rapidly, creeps back in.

We quit one thing only to get into a new situation where, at some point, we escape by quitting again. We become well versed, highly experienced but undisciplined quitters. Able to stand up tall, say *no* to the injustice and "the man" that is holding us down, and unapologetically stomp out the door, determined never to allow the imprisonment to occur again…until we find ourselves in yet another situation that we believe requires an escape.

Rarely do we ask ourselves questions like, "What is possible for me if I stay?" or "What is trying to come out of my blind spot and into my consciousness that has the potential to transform my entire experience of the world?" or "What parts of *me* will still be challenged even if I leave my current situation?"

If we ask these types of questions instead of being led by emotions of hopelessness, helplessness, and despair, we may be led into our greatest opportunity for growth and development. We may see the priceless gift that is waiting for us to tear open the wrapping paper and creatively use for our greatest good!

For example, you may think you need to quit your soul-sucking job to be in a better situation. But what if you can relax enough to see the gifts and lessons being afforded to you or see what is trying to emerge from within you by being there?

Perhaps, when you slow down and take on the creative approach of a Self-Leader, you realize that this job finances the thing you really want to create on the side, or it gives you access to training that will make it easier to find your next position, or it provides the health care benefits that you need in order to support your pregnant wife.

Maybe it is trying to teach you how to deal with difficult people, so when you finally leave and start your own business, you will have cut your teeth and messed up royally on someone else's dime.

Or it's even possible that it is giving you the chance to try out some strategies for creating better team dynamics and engagement in your "dysfunctional" department, so you will have a track record when you go off on your own and start consulting for small businesses with similar challenges.

When you can "fall in like" with your current position (in life or in work), you can treat that position as a creative endeavor instead of some torturous undertaking. This all starts with you being self-aware, present, attentive, and willing to flex your interpretations to what will serve and empower you instead of defaulting to a Prisoner reaction or conditioning.

Answering these questions will require you to be creative — to be a *creator* of a new story. Don't just consider the tangible things like money or training but also the intangible elements like persistence, character, confidence, and courage. If you eventually get to a point where you can truthfully say that there is nothing left to gain from your situation, then it may be time to move on from or remove that element from your life.

Once you have given the situation an honest look and have seen what gifts are present for you, the decision of whether or not to quit is no longer about trying to escape from discomfort, regardless of how mild or monumental that discomfort may feel at the moment. Instead, you can treat it as a choice to create the person, the feeling, or the impact you desire going forward.

It may end up that the outward action you take is the same. But when you slow things down and decide to quit as a means to build (instead of escape, avoid, or destroy), you can be free from the low-quality, heavy mechanisms of thought like worry, fear, resentment,

anger, and bitterness that may have been guiding your decisions and actions initially.

As a result, you will make choices from a place of flow instead of force and creation instead of avoidance. You will have more clarity and a higher level of consciousness, you will see the possibilities to be created, and you will be exercising true Self-Leadership in your life and your work.

Love and Light in the Real World

Attention is like a combination spotlight and vacuum cleaner: It illuminates what it rests upon and then sucks it into your brain-and your self.

—Rick Hanson

Being in the personal development world, I know quite a few deeply spiritual people who sign off each email, blog post, video, and even in-person hug with the phrase. "Love and Light."

They tell me they're sending me Love and Light or wishing me Love and Light or setting an intention for Love and Light.

What exactly it means, how they're sending it, and through what mechanism I'm supposed to receive it are still a bit of a mystery to me. But just as if I were in China and was bowed to while being greeted

in a foreign tongue, I know, based on the context, that the intention is a good one, meant to show care, warmth, and connection, and I am grateful for it. Plus, I'm a fan of anything that has an uplifting sound to it, so I don't really question it much.

Recently, though, this seemingly *woo-woo, airy-fairy, new-age* phrase, meant to send healing power and divine compassion through energy exchange—not much different from prayer or simple well wishes, I presume—took on a very active, practical, and creative meaning for me.

I was coaching a very successful young entrepreneur; we'll call him Kent, the co-founder of multiple seven-figure, highly regarded global technology companies, who had become a Prisoner of his own success.

He sought me out because he was craving a new challenge, something that would put him back in touch with what puts a fire in his belly; something that had been pushed down for too long, so he could focus on growing his company and growing himself. His sense was that a role where he was more of a public figure would excite him, but he was afraid of putting himself out there after being behind the scenes for so long. He felt paralysis around what would happen if he opened himself up, shared his uniqueness and what truly matters to him with the world, and it didn't "work out" or nobody cared about what he cared about.

Sorry to take a short detour, but I feel compelled to point out how beautiful and inclusive it feels to know that whether you're a well-to-do, successful entrepreneur like Kent, a CEO, someone who works a 9-5 job, or a college student getting ready to graduate and unleash yourself on the world, we all face similar challenges.

If you have ever felt stuck, unsure, or weighed down by a lack of clarity or certainty, or you have been afraid of stepping into a more powerful version of yourself for fear of judgment or a loss of love or support and the terror of some permanent, pervasive failure that would ruin your life, raise your hand.

Thank you for being honest. Just so you know, I'm raising my hand super high myself as I write this from a coffee shop.

We're all connected at a foundational level, and it feels good, at least to me, to know that we are not that special, in a very special way.

Back to my fearful, frozen, and a bit frenzied client. As happens quite often in my coaching, I wish I could simply hold up a technologically advanced mirror that would show him what I see in him—a man full of strength, creativity, ambition, and resourcefulness. But until NASA calls with the specs for the mirror, I needed something else to help him make a shift.

At that moment, the term *Love and Light* appeared in my head. It made me heavily question my intuition. Had I had one cup of kale-flavored Kombucha too many? What the heck was I supposed to do with that? Say it to him? I guessed that alone wouldn't serve him or help him make any movement on this particular challenge.

But then suddenly I got it.

Love and Light were not just some pleasant greeting that would surround my heart with a golden glow or cause me to touch my chest with my interlaced fingers. They were actually very practical tools to move him forward.

The first part of the equation is Love. I don't mean the love you have for your spouse or your children or your favorite pop star. I'm talking about capital "L" Love, which is the opposite of and the

antidote to fear. We don't need to overcome fear with willpower or strength; we simply need to bring in the presence of Love.

The way this showed up in my conversation with Kent was to have him start to ask himself the following question anytime these beliefs and stories arose about his next chapter: Will I respond to these thoughts from a place of Love or fear?

Fear is the easy one, but only because it is louder. Fear tries to convince us that something outside of us can either make us more whole or take away from our wholeness.

You may have chuckled a bit if you read that last sentence and noticed the inherent assumption that there are somehow *degrees of wholeness.* That would be like trying to create degrees of uniqueness. "Wow, that outfit is really unique" or in other words, "It is really one-of-a-kind!" Is there a way for something to be *sort of one-of-a-kind*?

Whole and unique are not up for interpretation. Just like your *enoughness,* your self-worth, and your value in the world—you are whole and unique without even having to try. It is only when we lose sight of that truth and are desperately trying to get back to something that never left us in the first place, that suffering is born.

When fear speaks in the language of consequences, missing out, or causing irreparable damage to our livelihood, it doesn't whisper; it roars. It booms like thunder, hoping that the sheer volume and force it brings will send us running for cover and succumbing to its will.

But what about Love? Love is the unsung hero and often-underestimated fighter (Lover?) in the battle. Love may not yell or scream, force or coerce, shame or belittle, but it is stronger in its understated articulation and presence than fear could ever hope to be.

It was clear to me that moving into a place of Love would be the quickest and most effective way to shift my client out of fear and into possibilities. Because when we give the heart some time, space, and a megaphone to speak its mind (and yes, the science of heart intelligence tells us that the heart does have a mind of its own), incredible things can happen.

At the depth of his biggest fears of not being enough, of taking imperfect action, of being debilitated by the possibility that people would no longer accept or approve of him, I invited him to try on a new possibility. I asked him, *"If you knew that you were always unconditionally loved and accepted, what would you do?"*

Breathing that question deep into his belly, I saw an immediate relaxation settle in. With each inhale of the possibility of living and creating—and creating from—this place of unconditional love, a corresponding exhale occurred, and with it the release of any further need to make decisions from fear.

Thinking about how to respond from a place of Love can often be enough to change everything, but my client was too smart for that. The smart ones are always the most resistant to change, so we needed something else to anchor this new awareness.

Luckily, I had one more trick up my sleeve—the second part of the equation, the Light. Where my spiritual friends may explain Light as a beautiful aura and an all-encompassing effervescence, I employed the Light from a very practical and pragmatic perspective.

My client's beliefs were being protected in the inner sanctum of his mind. They were being allowed to roam the hallways of his consciousness, setting up camp in any and every corner and crevice that they chose. There they would scurry about, unchallenged, unquestioned, and unsupervised, like cockroaches. Even worse,

creative cockroaches with an agenda; second only to the flying cockroaches I grew up with in Florida in the havoc they can wreak on your well-being!

What do cockroaches have to do with personal growth and overcoming fear? Well, what's the one thing that cockroaches hate — the thing that shakes them to their core and sends them running for their lives?

The Light.

By us simply flicking on the light switch, illuminating the dark and along with it the beliefs and assumptions that had convinced my client of his fragility and inability to do what he truly wanted, they started to scatter.

They had strength in numbers and anonymity, cloaked by darkness. But once we called them out, cornered them, and subjected them to a CIA / Mossad joint-task-force-style interrogation for proof and evidence to back up the rumors they had been spreading from the inside, their authority and influence were quickly eradicated, and they were rendered powerless.

In school, we were never taught how to — or that we even could — question and investigate our thoughts. We were never introduced to the idea that just because a thought exists, it does not make it true. Challenging these beliefs frees up the energy and creativity to create new ones.

It reminds me of the story by one of my favorite spiritual teachers, a woman who has had a profound effect on my life, Byron Katie. Her work, called "The Work," is one of the greatest tools I've ever seen to question your beliefs and bring about a powerful new sense of awareness.

In this particular story, she recalls when she came face-to-face with a deadly rattlesnake while hiking in the desert. Alone, powerless, and certain that her death was only moments away, she was filled with panic and fear. She knew that nobody would hear her cries for help and that she was doomed. As she tried to muster up the courage to run, she gave one last glance at the snake, only to realize it had been a coiled-up rope all along. She fell to her knees in laughter and tears.

One clear sign that your stories no longer have a hold on you and you have broken free from the prison of your mind is when you can think of the stories that once crippled you and laugh at their utter ridiculousness. The moment Katie knew she was safe, she could never un-see that what she thought was a poisonous beast, certain to kill her, was really a harmless, inanimate object that could never again manipulate or seduce her into a place of fear.

Fear is only present when there is an uninvestigated belief that arouses it. Unexamined thoughts are like oxygen for fear. If there is no belief, or you challenge the belief and meet it with understanding and compassion, there is no fear. Then, Love can show up more easily and with a more profound effect.

Your Love eradicates your fears, and your Light brings radiance to the dark.

From my most spiritual, logical, universal, and pragmatic place, I wish you not only Love and Light, but also the awareness of how to apply them in your world to truly be a Self-Leader.

The Turtle and the Life Preserver

> *Poor is the man whose pleasures depend on the permission of another.*
>
> —Madonna Ciccone

Where did I put that little ticket? Ah, there it is, right in my back pocket where I always keep it.

For the majority of my life, I walked around with this little metaphorical ticket that I would shove in the face of nearly everyone I met. I would hope and pray that one of them would be *the one* to validate me so I could finally leave the parking garage where I had been wandering aimlessly searching for my for self-worth. *"Make me worthy, oh great master, or friend, or family member, or boss, or cute girl at the bar, or barista who I told a joke to that kinda missed the mark!"*

That's not the way it looks when we're actually in it, of course.

When we approach the world and our proof of self-worth from a Prisoner-centric system of thoughts, even when someone stamps our ticket and we are ecstatic, it doesn't last for long. And how could it?

A simple vocabulary lesson tells us exactly why this is the case. Walk up to any child (preferably one you know so as not to be hauled off for questioning or banned from your local grocery store) and ask them to point at them *self*. I guarantee that 10 out of 10 of them would point correctly.

At some point, though, we decided that someone other than our self could best handle the measurement of our self-worth. So if we can't trust ourselves to see how exceptional we are, we may as well just ask every friend and family member and stranger for that validation and that love and that acceptance instead. Are you laughing at the insanity of it all yet?

Have you ever thought about how freeing it would feel to really be yourself and to share all the best, silliest, weirdest, most passionate parts of you without worrying whether or not people would love and accept you in all of your unapologetic glory? If you haven't, take a minute to do that now.

Does it feel incredible and absolutely impossible at the same time? If it doesn't seem like it is a reality you could ever experience, it's only because you are *believing* a thought that is creating that limitation. That thought is not based on any real truth. Instead, it is based on what you *think* you know to be true in this moment—the unchallenged *truth*, which is the only thing that ever truly holds us back.

To start questioning what is currently "true" for you, I invite you to ask yourself what you would need to know was true instead for that type of *radical self-acceptance* to be a real possibility for you.

When I asked myself this question, I discovered that if I knew that being loving and trusting myself was the most direct path to experiencing validation and acceptance, from the inside-out, then I would start living and playing full out right now. It doesn't mean that I necessarily have to believe that to be true in this moment because when I choose Self-Leadership, it means I am willing to simply experiment and test to see if that *new truth* could be just as true, if not more true, than my original belief.

When I introduce people to what I call *"evidence-based belief shifting,"* where they don't have to agree with, believe in, or be convinced of anything but instead test it and find the evidence for themselves where it is true, they tend to get really excited. They start questioning their long-held truths and beliefs—which often times are not even their own but inherited from family, friends, or some other type of conditioning—and instantly start feeling a sense of Self-Leadership, lightness, possibilities, and personal power.

For some people, though, access to this type of power brings up new thoughts of whether they deserve the freedom that it affords. They sometimes think that Self-Leadership, in particular the part of Self-Leadership that allows us to be a leader in our thinking and truth-seeking, is something that only really "special" people can (or should) have access to.

They are absolutely right. Self-Leadership *is* for a special kind of person. So let's run a little experiment to see if you are, in fact, *special enough* to be a Self-Leader and deserving enough to experience true and long-lasting freedom, fulfillment, and happiness.

It has been said that the probability of you being who you are, born where you were born to your parents, and living the life you are living right now is *one in 400 trillion!*

Not impressive enough of a statistic for you? Then try this one on for size.

Dr. Ali Binazir once wrote about the Buddhist version of this one-in-400 trillion probability that he calls *precious incarnation.* Dr. Binazir describes precious incarnation like this:

Imagine there was one life preserver thrown somewhere in some ocean, with exactly one turtle in all of these oceans, swimming underwater somewhere. The probability that you came about is the same as that turtle sticking its head out of the water—into the middle of that life preserver. On one try.

And though it may sound like I am trying to convince you of your worthiness with anecdotes, math, statistics, and probabilities, I'm actually trying to activate something deeper. I'm trying to get you to see that you are *worthy,* just by being on this Earth, being able to breathe this air, having the ability to read this book. It isn't some coincidence that of all the things you could be, you are you. From this place, it is easy to develop a deep knowing that you are, without a doubt or question, worthy.

Still not convinced of your inherent worthiness? Think you need more proof? I like to relate our worthiness to gravity. Gravity is present and active whether you believe in it or not. No matter how passionate of an argument someone might present to you, it would not likely faze you. In fact, you could test it out by disavowing gravity right now. I'll wait.

Are you still in your chair? You didn't float away into the cosmos like a balloon in the hands of an easily distracted child? Whew, glad that worked out in both of our favors.

It's not about believing in yourself because if you believe in something, you can also un-believe in it. It's about knowing. It's about a true understanding. It's about seeing that in every step you take, whether you notice it or not, you're experiencing gravity. And at the same time, you're also experiencing worthiness, being good enough, being deserving.

This doesn't mean you won't continue to learn, develop, and evolve; it's just that your growth becomes a bonus to the already perfect existence that you experience moment-by-moment. When you see the world through the lens of Self-Leadership, you know that you are both the artist and the work of art at every step of your journey.

Artists can mold a block of clay into a statue, but they can stop at any point, and simply because they had a hand in molding the block, it is, in and of itself a work of art. Could it be more pronounced? Could it be different? Could it be more detailed or focused? Sure, but it doesn't have to be. Nothing would make it more or less worthy, more or less of a work of art, if it were.

My friend and fellow coach, the late, great Michelle Bauman once told me, *"Your worthiness cannot be put on a dimmer switch."* Neither you nor anyone else can increase or decrease it.

Instead of trying to find or force validation from the outside in, you can honor yourself for who you are, the artist and the masterpiece, the one-in-400-trillion human being, the turtle in the life preserver, while being open to a playful state of evolution (because you *get to* not because you *have to*) and a focus on the possibilities that can be created when you see just how incredible you truly are.

The Truth About Roller Coasters

---

life should not be a journey to the grave with the intention of arriving safely in a pretty and well preserved body, but rather to skid in broadside in a cloud of smoke, thoroughly used up, totally worn out, and loudly proclaiming 'Wow! What a Ride!!!'

—Hunter S. Thompson

---

1 in 750 million. That is the chance of being fatally injured on a roller coaster.

1 in 24 million. That is the likelihood of being injured seriously enough to need overnight hospitalization.

I looked up these figures after a coaching session with a client who was venting about how growing her business felt like being on an *emotional roller coaster*. What she meant was what most people mean when they equate this "terrifying" carnival ride to their life situations—an intense and unpredictable ride filled with uncertainty, fear, and the potential for sickness and even death (or more accurately, the loss of something; freedom, security, happiness, etc.).

Most people who know me well know that I am constantly questioning the language we use (including my own) because I believe doing so can shift beliefs that we have held to be true for so long—beliefs that may be keeping us in a false, self-imposed state of Prisoner-ness. Though I had never felt the desire to question this particular analogy before, as soon as she brought it up, I instantly wondered if there was any truth to how we typically use it.

If we dive a bit deeper, a roller coaster is a very fitting and comforting analogy for life (and in my client's case, her business). Roller coasters are not some flung-together piece of metal with no thought or consideration put into them.

Brilliant minds and meticulous engineers have crafted them, safety-conscious teams of professionals have assembled them, and vigilant technicians regularly and thoroughly check them. Though we don't have a crew of people crafting our lives (thank goodness!), I do believe we have a "team" of sorts. This team is a mixture of our gifts, experiences, brilliance, intuition, creative intelligence, and whatever higher power or level of consciousness that fits within your belief system, that are all conspiring to help us create what we want most in our lives.

Beyond my interpretation of the support structure we have at our disposal at all times, I also believe there are some real gifts to

living life on a roller coaster. Roller coasters are designed to deliver predictable periods of discomfort and excitement, moments of terror and joy. They follow a very purposeful trajectory, sometimes starting off calmly and slowly before screaming down the track into a 180-degree loop, then soaring into the sky and plunging back down towards earth, all before pulling safely into the station to be reset and launched again.

The scariest time we ride a roller coaster will always be the first time. And while it may feel like we are boarding a new roller coaster for the first time every time we try something new, when we choose to be Self-Leaders and embrace the ride, we will quickly see that the still stages and the scary stages are never permanent. They are all phases of planned (by whom or what doesn't matter) discomfort and unpredictability. The sooner we see that, the sooner we can enjoy being hurled at the ground at 100 miles per hour and the sooner we can trust the intelligence behind the plan to slow us down at the perfect moment and keep us safe regardless of how far outside of our comfort zone we are leaning.

We may not have control over the twists, turns, and drops, but we can choose to use them as an excuse to throw our hands up in the air, laugh (and maybe scream sometimes), and enjoy the ride.

Stories Versus Misunderstandings

> *Any intelligent fool can make things bigger, more complex. It takes a touch of genius–and a lot of courage–to move in the opposite direction.*
>
> —Albert Einstein

In the world of personal growth, we often talk about how our stories are what create our world. They are one of the reasons that we *do have* something we *don't want* or that we *don't have* something we *do want*. So it stands to reason that rewriting those stories is the best way to finally be happy, fulfilled, and prosperous. Sometimes though, the stories are so deeply ingrained that I focus my attention elsewhere to develop a new perspective.

In an attempt to *uncomplicate* and *un-Prisoner-ize* what it takes to experience transformation in our lives, when talking about long-

standing, limiting beliefs that are holding me back, I have started replacing the word *stories* with the word *misunderstandings*. It is my belief that by focusing on the *simple fundamental misunderstandings* (or SFMs as I call them) we may have about the way the world works, we remove the notion that optimizing our lives has to include deep, intensely painful work done over the course of several decades in order to be effective. Instead, it can start now, at this very moment!

Imagine, for example, that after all these years of hearing the "story" of *Goldilocks and the Three Bears*, some marketing genius decided to reboot the story to make it more relatable. "We are going to recast Goldilocks as a female bodybuilder. An endangered species of buffalo from Botswana will replace the three bears. And instead of porridge, the Quinoa Association of America have offered a generous sponsorship to have their much sexier grain in the bowl. Do you think anyone will notice? Do you think they will care?"

Yes, I think everyone will notice, and everyone will care! Getting people to forget what they have always known about *Goldilocks and the Three Bears* and replacing it with this new story is going to take a lot of time and work, and it will certainly be met with a lot of resistance!

The same resistance can happen when we try to rewrite the conditioning, the patterns, the beliefs, and the stories that we believe have driven our feelings, our behavior, and our success up to this point. They just seem too heavy, too permanent, too far beyond reinvention.

A misunderstanding, on the other hand, feels lighter and more innocent. It sounds like something that can be painlessly understood and easily shifted to a new way of seeing (and being in) the world.

"Did you say you want me to pick you up at 7:30?"

"No, actually I said 7:15."

"Oh, sorry for the *misunderstanding*; 7:15 it is!"

If there were a formula for an SFM, it would go something like this: *"I thought I was struggling with X, but really, it was a simple misunderstanding about Y."*

For example, one of my clients, a CEO and serial entrepreneur who has launched several successful companies with the same group of partners, was struggling with worry and anxiety, thinking that she wouldn't have the same level of success if she started something new without them. But really, she had a simple misunderstanding that her partners were the cause of her success instead of seeing that it was in large part due to her gift for picking people with complimentary skill sets, being able to tap into her innate creativity, and her consistent and diligent work ethic, that made those ventures so profitable.

Another one of my clients thought her suffering in situations where things didn't "work out" came from the situations themselves. But really, she had a simple misunderstanding about the permanence and pervasiveness of those situations in her life. Once she saw that any setback she experienced was nothing more than a temporary, isolated information point that yielded valuable data for how to move forward, the suffering melted away.

Yet another client thought that when he was uncertain or overwhelmed, the pressure he felt meant that he was on the path to failure or that he wasn't cut out to create the business he had dreamed of. But really, he had a simple misunderstanding that those feelings said something about him or his abilities instead of the truth that those feelings were merely gentle reminders from his

brain's "early detection system" to tell him that slowing down in that moment and asking himself what was trying to emerge from within him was his most effective course of action.

These are just a few of countless examples of SFMs from which my clients and I created an "a-ha" in the course of a single conversation. Notice, we didn't have to fix anything in these situations. We simply worked together to help them understand what was going on. And when they did, things immediately began to change because they saw the role they could play in changing them. Not because they had to, but because they got to!

None of these clients needed to have deep therapy over the course of years, sell all of their possessions and move to an ashram in India, or beat themselves up because they misunderstood in the first place. Because with a new understanding comes purposeful, relaxed, and creative new options for growing businesses, strengthening relationships, loving ourselves, and any number of other things that we previously didn't believe we could make happen—or least not without force, anxiety, and pressure.

Did it take some time for these new understandings to stick? Sometimes, and that is only natural.

But for most, it doesn't take long to adopt the new understanding at an almost unconscious level through gentle reminders from within and consistent practice. After a short time, it becomes as ingrained in them as when they walk outside in the evening and see that it's dark. They don't have to remember a 5-step system to overcome the sun's absence or meditate on why it is no longer light out. It's nighttime, so it's dark. It's simple, nothing to process or remember once they understand what is really going on in the world.

Being aware of these simple fundamental misunderstandings—especially noticing that that is all they are, not some quarter-century old story that we have to attack and purge from our system—opens us to use our power as Self-Leaders to develop a new way of being and doing that supports that new understanding.

Living and practicing those insights moment-by-moment anchors them inside of us and helps us integrate them into our daily lives so we can create what we desire instead of wasting our precious energy and creative brainpower on remediation or rehabilitation.

How to Organ-Ize
Your Lightning

There are no rules and regulations for perfect composition. If there were we would be able to put all the information into a computer and would come out with a masterpiece. We know that's impossible. You have to compose by the seat of your pants.

—Arnold Newman

"When thunder roars, go indoors." That was the advice I heard on the news recently when there was a storm heading my way. It makes logical sense. After all, a lightning strike can be deadly, and its unpredictability and unrestrained power are reasonable causes for concern.

But not everyone hunkers down in the face of unfathomable and skin-frying levels of energy. Doc Brown from the *Back to the Future* movie trilogy (and FYI, this will not be the only *Back to the Future* reference in this book) took a different approach.

He had the idea that if he could harness, purposefully focus, and orchestrate the path of the electricity that the lightning made available to him (whether he asked for it or not), could be used to create the impossible—1.21 gigawatts of impossible to be exact.

The truth is that each of us has access to 1.21 gigawatts of energy inside of us. We just may not know how to shape it, so it ends up feeling like unfocused, hopeless, stressful anxiety! This is energy management in the Prisoner's world—frantic and unyielding.

George Carlin once said, "Electricity is really just organized lightning."

Now, Carlin is also the guy who said, "Frisbeetarianism is the belief that when you die, your soul goes up on the roof and gets stuck," but let's humor him nonetheless.

It sounds like a wild contradiction doesn't it; "organized lightning?" How can you organize something as chaotic and random as lightning?

The same glaring contradiction shows up when we think about trying to organize our own frantic, messy, and overwhelming feelings. If we define *organize* as to control by force or construct certainty around, we most likely won't be able to do it, at least not without leaking energy and exhausting ourselves mentally and emotionally.

But what if we experiment with a new definition of the word, written as *organ-ize.*

The root of *organize* is *organ*, as in an instrument. A tool that, when properly used, allows us to create beautiful music. When you think about it, instruments are the only way anything meaningful has even been created by (wo)man.

Pianos, guitars, voices, hearts, and minds—these are all instruments to fully express our unique perspectives, our convictions, our deepest love, and our truest selves.

When you choose Self-Leadership and intentionally *organ-ize* your lightning, you convert it from a frenzied and disorderly ball of scattered energy, desires, doubts, fears, and ideas into a work of art, a piece of music, your own personal masterpiece.

Self-Leaders do this by becoming *conductors*, in two different ways.

First, you become the conductor of the electricity (the lightning) available to you. You are the conduit that is able to pick up and allow that energy to flow. In physics, the best conductors are those that give very little resistance to the flow of that energy. That, too, is your goal as the conductor of your organized lightning; not allowing resistance to stop you from being in flow.

And the easiest way to not allow resistance to hold you back is to not be in resistance to your resistance. I know, it sounds like doubletalk, but what I'm inviting you to do is notice the resistance you are feeling, thank it for showing up and teaching you whatever it thinks you need to learn, and then just allow it to *be* without trying to force it out. It will get bored and leave when it's not getting the attention it thinks it deserves.

The next step is to become the type of conductor who leads an orchestra. You don't necessarily play or have control over the instruments.

You simply direct the activity; you feel the music and the energy coming through you and put your full attention on your role in creating a beautiful, cohesive, and powerful piece of music. The energy comes *to you* and then the energy flows *through you*. You don't have to summon it, look for it, coax it, or even ask for it. It is a gift that you wake up with every morning and have access to throughout the day.

And whether your "impossible" is time traveling like Doc Brown, writing a book, having more success in your business, deepening your relationships or choosing happiness, know that the instruments you need to do each are tuned and waiting for you to organ-ize and orchestrate their use in the way that only you can.

What will you do with *your* lightning?

Difficulty Is Part of the Game

When you improve a little each day, eventually big things occur.... Not tomorrow, not the next day, but eventually a big gain is made. Don't look for the big, quick improvement. Seek the small improvement one day at a time. That's the only way it happens—and when it happens, it lasts.

—John Wooden

I posted the quote above by John Wooden on one of my social media profiles one day and, within minutes, someone (an accomplished professional working in a corporate environment) responded to the post saying: "Difficult to do in this instant gratification culture we live in... but a necessary reminder!"

It got me thinking, and she was absolutely right. We do live in an instant gratification culture.

But there was another word that stuck out to me in her reply. The word was *difficult*.

Seeing difficulty as a deterrent to something meaningful is one of the reasons why the instant gratification culture exists to begin with. Think about it: If we see an option that both is non-difficult and allows us to win now, why would we ever choose the difficult option and the accompanying results that occur over time?

Difficulty is actually a very worthwhile element for mastery of anything worth doing and, interestingly enough, is a major design element in the video game world.

What if, in the real world much like in video games, instead of being a Prisoner to it, trying to avoid discomfort at all costs, or viewing challenge as a barrier to success, difficulty was simply a part of the game?

I've never really been into video games myself, but hardcore gamers have told me that if the games were easy, they would get bored and move on to something else. It is the existence of harder levels, bigger obstacles, and the huge sense of victory when you conquer them that keep these vigilant *digi-warriors* focused and engaged!

This is what separates the dogged determination of the *plucky players* from the casual carelessness of the *joystick jockeys*. The *dabblers* want a pleasant distraction or a quick sense of completion — whichever they can accomplish with the least amount of effort. The real gamers, Self-Leaders on their quest for mastery and excellence, crave a challenge. They love going around that blind corner in the virtual reality battlefield and being blown to smithereens.

Yes, it does mean they have to start over. But the next time they trek out into that war zone, they have a definite edge over the competition because their time doing the sometimes difficult (and ultimately rewarding) work and *failing forward* is what increases their ability to anticipate and respond to the unexpected while also growing their focus and reflexes. As a result, they also greatly increase their chance for success as they transition from the seemingly impossible to the consistently achievable.

If *meaning* is what you are looking to create, then just for today, choose difficult over instant, uncertainty over safety, and advanced over beginner. And choose it as a creative, curious, and resilient player in this opportunity-filled game of life. It may just make the difficult, easy.

Game on!

Always and Never-Never Land

> The limits of my language means
> the limits of my world.
>
> —Ludwig Wittgenstein

I can trace my fascination with language back to my days as a rapper—yes, I was a rapper! Intricate, often humorous, multi-syllable wordplay, metaphors, analogies, and plays on words were what I was known for. So paying close attention to language was something I developed a curiosity about and skill for.

My fascination with language has carried forward into my speaking, training, and coaching. It is a core part of how I help my clients and the audiences I speak to move past the lies, myths, and misunderstandings they have been conditioned to believe. Whether they created these beliefs themselves or well-intentioned farmers planted them there at some point in their lives, these stories play out daily—or multiple times per day—in the language they choose to describe the world they live in.

I believe so strongly in the power of language and am so intrigued by how it paints our experience of the world that being vigilant and hyper aware of the words my clients use to "speak" their world has become a game! It is a game because I have seen firsthand in their lives, and certainly in my own, how ridiculously fun it can be to change the rules we follow and the language we use to immediately start to transform many areas of our lives!

Two words that turn me into whatever the equivalent of a bomb-sniffing dog is for seeing where people may be stuck in a Prisoner-perspective (and thus have an opportunity to instantly break free) are *always* and *never*.

"I always do this." "Things never work out." "It always seems like something goes wrong." "I could never do that."

Always and *never* are absolute, fixed, permanent, and unchangeable. They reference the past but are carried forward into the future as if they were a diagnosis.

That *self-misdiagnosis* is dangerous input for our brains' operating system. The brain is significantly affected when it hears us proclaim: "This is the way things always (or never) happen, so why would anything change?"

Choosing more empowering language is not about the *power of positive thinking* or lying to ourselves. It is a reflection of the truth. It is language that is created and rooted in the present moment and reflects the facts of our reality much more than the pervasive labels of *always* and *never* possibly could.

Instead of defaulting to *always* and *never*, isn't it more truthful (and less shameful, blameful, and constricting) to say things like "historically," "up to this point," or "in the past I did/didn't do/was challenged by ABC or XYZ"?

As you read this, you may be thinking that it's too simple and can't make a difference to choose such a small shift in your language. But I'm not asking you to believe in what I'm saying or trust in it or anything else that has you do something out of a sense of blind faith or compliance. I simply invite you to test it out for yourself.

If you catch yourself using absolute words like *always* and *never*, take a pause and ask yourself whether you can know with certainty that something will *always* or *never* happen a certain way in the future. If the answer is no, you don't know for sure that it will *always* or *never* be that way, why not try out a different, more realistic choice of words to create an interpretation of the situation at hand that is more accurate and less catastrophic?Self-Leadership involves practicing the skill of being truthful about the challenges you face—not making it worse than it is and not sweeping it under the rug and ignoring it. Prisoners see their setbacks as permanent and pervasive—"Losing this job means I will never find another (permanent), and it also means I am going to lose everything else I hold dear (pervasive)."

Self-Leaders have an entirely different explanatory style in these situations. They are self-aware and know the reality, which is that setbacks are temporary ("There is no correlation between losing this job and finding another") and isolated ("No longer working at this company has no direct connection to a loss in any other part of my life").

What seems like an elementary exercise in semantics will start to transform your thinking, and you will recognize that there are no habits, stories, beliefs, or ways of being or doing of which you must be a Prisoner.

By making this shift, you will have given yourself permission to reinvent yourself starting right now. You will have recaptured

your sense of Self-Leadership, your internal power, and can now confidently say that it doesn't matter what you did or what happened to you (or more accurately *for you*) five years ago, five weeks ago, five days ago, or even five minutes ago. All of that is in the past and is an unemotional data point of information that you must welcome without resistance or struggle if you are to create something new in its place in the future.

Remember, you have the creative power and the spirit of ownership to change who you are being and what you are doing in an instant—not because you must or have to or because something is wrong, but just because you can, you get to and because it's fun!

At 87 MPH Marty Gets Killed by the Libyans

*Ambition is the path to success.
Persistence is the vehicle you arrive in.*

—Bill Bradley

If you didn't get the reference in the title, it may mean we can't be friends. It comes from one of my favorite movies of all time, the epic *Back to the Future* trilogy (I told you earlier that there would be at least a couple BttF references in this book)!

The star of the movie is the flux-capacitor-equipped DeLorean car that, when it hits a speed of 88 miles per hour, can travel through time! Not 85 or 86 or 87 miles per hour, but 88!

The first time we see the vehicle do its magical thing, the main character, Marty (played by the young, talented and very '80s Michael J. Fox), is trying to escape from a group of bazooka-wielding Libyan terrorists in a mall parking lot. As he is weaving through

the lot trying to avoid certain death, he eventually hits 88 MPH, and the DeLorean instantly transports him back in time and out of harm's way!

I tell you this story not because I love to recount '80s movies as a hobby (okay maybe a little), but because there is an important lesson here about something called *activation energy*.

Activation energy is the point at which a chemical (or any other transformative) reaction occurs, resistance is overcome, and momentum and results are accelerated. It can come from steady improvement and also from intense bursts of purposeful, creative, and focused action.

It doesn't always look like a volcanic eruption or a power plant meltdown though. It is often small, incremental, and seemingly insignificant, but it makes all the difference in the world.

It's why at 211 degrees, water is hot, but at 212 degrees it boils.

It's why some paper can easily withstand 450 degrees of heat but bursts into flames at 451.

And it's why at 87 miles per hour, Marty would have been blown to smithereens by the Libyans who wanted their stolen plutonium back but at 88 miles per hour, he went on the adventure of a lifetime, traveling through time, taking his mother to prom and winning the hearts of movie-goers across the world.

Right now, you may be thinking that you have been working tirelessly on a new business or trying to build a stronger relationship with your spouse or trying to get in shape, and you are ready to scrap all of it. I hear you, I do. I've been there, I've felt it, and at times, I've given in to it.

But before you give in and give up, know this: The way you find *your* activation energy—the one degree that separates where you are from where you want to be—is to *stay on the path*. Whatever that path is. Sincerely devoted, highly involved, and with low or no attachment to a specific outcome looking a specific way.

The examples of activation energy I shared with you were not found by intellectualizing or waiting or hoping; they were found *by doing* – by being in action.

Discoveries like these, in our own lives, are created by choosing Self-Leadership and purposeful action in this moment and then choosing it again the next moment, and the next moment, and the moment after that. Not as a means to an end but as a means to continue.

Those who succeed, those who stay consistent, diligent, committed but also relaxed and playful and have fun with the process will end up meeting their activation energy when they least expect it.

Where will you lovingly and sincerely commit to continuing to be in action, with no attachment to an outcome or a timeline of when "it" should/must/needs to happen?

You may be only one mile per hour, one email, one phone call, one green smoothie, one investor pitch, one difficult conversation, one workout, one blog post, or one date night away from finding, meeting, and thriving inside of your own activation energy and being truly unstoppable.

Have No More Than One Bad Day per Week

I am not what happened to me,
I am what I choose to become.

—C.G. Jung

"You can't be serious, kid!" This was my response when reading the following passage in a 20+ page leadership development plan that a 22-year-old, ambitious MBA student had submitted for a leadership competition where I was a judge a few years ago:

"Further, to ensure that I have a greater sense of joy, less conflict, and the best possible chance for success in my personal and professional endeavors going forward, *I plan on having no more than one bad day per week.*"

My first thought when reading it was to find him, pat him on the head, and in my most nurturing voice (which I'm guessing would

be hard to distinguish from blatantly condescending), cradle him and tell him what a sweet boy he was.

I finished reading the rest of his paper, still smirking because of my brilliance and enlightenment I'm sure, and then I set it aside and moved onto the next candidate.

About four pages into the next student's submission, I realized I was no longer paying attention to the lessons they reported learning about self-awareness, their greatest weaknesses, or how the DiSC assessment nailed their personality type. I was still stuck on what that innocent and inexperienced tenderfoot of the world had intellectualized about his future bad days.

What initially sounded like giggle-worthy naivety quickly became a simple and powerful reminder of our ability to choose, as the Self-Leaders of our experiences, what our days will look like. He was taking a true inner stance of Self-Leadership by deciding just how often he would choose to have a bad day. It is really no different than having *"Taco Tuesday"* with our family or a weekly staff meeting at work. If we can choose when those events occur, why not also choose, ahead of time, how we will approach our daily lives?

We are conscious creators of each and every moment of our lives as well as our responses to circumstances and outcomes in any given situation. So while I wouldn't make it a practice to predetermine that certain days will be "bad" ones, I would invite you to consider that every day starts with a neutrality, an innocence, and a blank canvas of possibilities on which you choose what to paint and what your masterpiece for that day will look like.

Take a minute now, irrespective of what time it is, regardless of what else you have on your schedule, and no matter how you

may have started your day, to choose how the rest of your day will unfold.

If you are willing to be open to the possibilities and not be a Prisoner to the situations or circumstances that may arise today— the people, problems, and predicaments that you have no control over—you have everything you need to be the person who creates a great day instead of waiting for a great day to be created for you.

Oh, and if you are reading this, young man, thank you for providing a shining example of Self-Leadership. I won't take it personally if you pat *me* on the head the next time we see each other.

You Say You Can't Do It... And I Agree!

Whether you think you can, or you think you can't—you're right.

—Henry Ford

Once Self-Leaders shift their problems into projects, they know exactly what action they need to take. But even then, what often happens is that a little bit of Prisoner creeps in and shouts, "But I can't do that!"

When clients of mine want to start or grow a business, have a difficult conversation with their spouse or boss, or do anything else that they feel is overflowing with uncertainty, and they default to "I can't do that," I know exactly where to go next.

This may seem highly untraditional, but instead of an obligatory rah-rah session to pump them up and psyche them out, I will often

agree with them. I tell them I believe them. When they tell me they can't do something, I know that it's true.

They can't do it based on who they are *being* right now. They're scared, they're emotional, or they're afraid of rejection. Fine. This version of them can't do it.

But I firmly know that there is a version inside of them that can do it. So I ask them, "Who would you need to *be* to make this happen?" I will often challenge them to create a physical list to answer that question.

I have my own list for me as well. Some of the versions of me that I need to be, the qualities I must choose to embody, in order to show up as my best self include patient, focused, relaxed, unattached to outcomes, playful, light, creative, not-so-serious, selfless, rested, and courageous. As soon as I saw that these were conscious choices and not some hereditary advantage or deficiency, I was able to show up as that person whenever I wanted to with much less effort!

One fun and simple way to embody your "who" once you know what that looks like, comes from a game that my coach Steve Chandler taught me when I was certain that I couldn't do something. He called it the "Robot Game." I use it all the time myself and with my clients, and I even have a little robot toy to remind me of it.

The robot game is a tool you can use anytime you need to do something that you feel you (or again, more accurately, *this* version of you) are not suited to do. It could be something in your personal life or business, a challenge at school or work, an uncomfortable situation that you have to have a conversation about, a sales call, or anything else.

No matter the challenge, when you play the Robot Game, it doesn't matter if you are not "that kind of person," if you are too

afraid, too doubtful, or too insecure because *you* are not the one who is going to take on the task. Whatever it is you need to do, you just "give it to the robot!"

This robot is quite simply just a version of you that has all of your strengths, abilities, experiences, and power. But it has none of that pesky emotional attachment to the particular meaning of the situation, what the outcome says about you as a person, and whether or not you're good enough, deserve it or can make it happen. All the robot version of you does, is what you tell it to do.

If there is something I have to do, for example, reach out to a prospective client, and I'm afraid of coming across as pushy or salesy, looking bad, not being good enough, and not saying the right thing, I can ask the robot to make the call. I'll say, "Hey, robot, call John and tell him that you want to meet with him because you have some creative ideas on how to help him grow his business."

And the robot says, "Sure thing, sounds like fun! What's his number? I'll call him right now."

The robot doesn't care about any of that self-doubt, approval-seeking or worthiness crap. He doesn't care how he looks. He's simply programmed to do a job, and he does it. Then, once he has done the "hard part" for me, I can dive back in with all of my greatness, enthusiasm, genius, and desire to serve and do the things that I love doing.

The Robot Game allows us to bypass taking our emotional temperature and get into purposeful action! Self-Leaders are always looking for creative ways to live a more effective and fun life, and this game is our imagination in full effect.

Sometimes people will ask me, "But isn't this just tricking ourselves to perform certain tasks by pretending we are a robot?"

To which I respond, "Absolutely!" It is a mind trick, a mind shift, a total fabrication. So is everything else in our lives—both the tricks that serve us and the tricks that don't.

The Prisoners go along with the story written for them. They go through the motions and never challenge or question the path or the results. The Self-Leaders know they have full control over writing their own story.

Since it is all made up, we have the choice to invent a story that helps us to be empowered and inspired instead of paralyzed and devastated. Put the robot on speed dial; he will quickly become your best friend or your highest performing employee!

The End in Mind, Not the End in Stone

The art of living...is neither careless drifting on the one hand nor fearful clinging to the past on the other. It consists in being sensitive to each moment, in regarding it as utterly new and unique, in having the mind open and wholly receptive.

—Alan W. Watts

Stephen Covey, in his book *The 7 Habits of Highly Effective People*, talks about how we should "begin with the end in mind." This is great advice and is based on the belief that we create everything twice; first in the mind and then in the physical world.

For many of us, somewhere along the way, the meaning changed from a place of visualizing the possibilities to a place where we have

to know exactly what our path will look like five years from now before we take a single step.

Five years!? I'm not even sure what I'm having for dinner tonight!

There is nothing wrong with having a plan or an intention or an idea of where you want to go. In fact, there is nothing wrong with a detailed plan, unless it comes from fear.

Fear-based planning will restrict your creativity because it closes off your imagination and redirects that energy to the misguided belief that there is something you can do to guarantee a certain outcome. When we plan from fear, our creativity is held Prisoner, our hearts and souls drop out of the process, and our analytical mind with its memory- and experience-based limitations hijack the show.

What if you instead of making a step-by-step plan that is supposed to map out each step of your journey from where you are standing now to where you will lie for eternity, you envisioned what an average day in your life would look like? A vivid picture of how you want to feel when you wake up and when you go to sleep, what you want to create, and whom you want to serve.

Create space for this introspection and let it be as loose or specific as it occurs to you to be. No need to force yourself to be overly vague or overly rigid. Just let whatever comes to mind be there and write it down as it does.

Then, be sincerely and playfully committed to living in a way that helps you achieve that vision, but be unattached to having it look any particular way. A strong commitment to that *created future* will pull you toward your goals while allowing you the flexibility to make small course corrections along the way.

You can still create a plan, even a detailed roadmap, if it excites you and sparks your enthusiasm to do so. But please don't allow your fear to hold your spirit and creative energy hostage by believing the thought that you have to know all the right answers, especially before you even truly know the right questions.

The Rules Don't Apply to You

If you obey all the rules, you miss all the fun.
—Katharine Hepburn

A client of mine who I'll call Michael, an accomplished, energetic, and difference-making entrepreneur, wanted to grow a new area of his business but was struggling.

It wasn't because of a lack of capability or value in the services he provides. His belief of all of the rules he had to follow in order to be successful caused the struggle. These weren't laws or regulations that he had a legal, moral, or ethical obligation to follow. They were simply assumptions and limitations he placed on himself based on what he saw everyone else doing and believing it was a requirement for him to do the same. He had become a Prisoner to the rules that were not only keeping him stuck, but also squelching access to his natural creative abilities.

In this weak and yet pushy part of his mind, his thoughts about not being prominent enough in his community, that he hated

networking events, and that he didn't have an elaborate Internet marketing sales funnel were treated as much more significant than the mere data points of information that they were. They were the equivalent of a huge iron gate, 100 feet tall, surrounded by electrified barbed wire, separating him from what he wanted. There was no way out but to climb up and over it and potentially fall and fail in the process. No wonder he was stuck!

The challenge here had nothing to do with the rules themselves, but that he believed the rules applied to him!

It reminds me of a viral video I saw some time ago. In a news report from New Jersey, video captured how a big steel fence stopped the FBI in their tracks by when they were conducting a raid on a house. The fence appeared locked, so the first agent in tried climbing over it. Though he struggled and it seemed both painful and awkward, he eventually made it over.

What made this video so humorous was that just after he made it to the other side, the next two FBI agents realized the fence wasn't locked and simply pushed it opened and walked right through. They didn't thoughtlessly follow the first agent's path just because he came before them; they ignored that "rule" and took an easier and more direct route.

Where in your life can you step into being an effective Self-Leader instead of an affected Prisoner and walk directly through the door of opportunity without placing unneeded barriers in your path? All barriers, rules, conditions, and requirements are invented anyway—for better or for worse. So why not invent ones that move you forward into creative action?

For example, my client hated networking because he believed the "rule" that it had to be an exercise in speed dating and *forcible*

business card deployment. However, he was great at connecting with people when he brought them together into a space where he controlled the pace and flow and where he was responsible for setting the context and the conditions of the game. Why should this be any different?

He also loathed the rule of only reaching out to people when he had something to sell them but loved having meaningful conversations with people to deepen his relationships with them and see how he could make their lives better.

When he made the shift from viewing the rules as a barrier to seeing them as a starting point for creative exploration, he realized that he would never again have to blindly follow what others had demonstrated as "the" path.

He was able to zoom out, slow down, tap into his unique gifts, and make up his own rules based on what he wanted to create and in the way that was most in alignment with what created a high-spirited sense of enthusiasm inside of him.

When you own the process of creating those rules, you are in love with them, and you give yourself permission to do what you do best instead of setting up unnecessary brick walls that you end up pounding your head against.

The best illustration I have ever seen on the power of creating and owning your rules comes from a Zen koan, a puzzling riddle of sorts used in the practice of Zen Buddhism that typically has no "correct" answer.

One of these koans depicts a scenario where a baby goose is placed in a bottle with his neck and head guided to the opening at the top of the bottle. From that time on, the goose is fed and nourished, causing its body to grow to a point that it is forever stuck in this

glass fortress with just its head and neck continuing to protrude through the top of the bottle.

The question posed in the riddle is this: How do you get the goose out of the bottle without breaking these two rules: Rule one, you cannot kill the goose and, Rule two, you cannot break the bottle.

Students would hear this story and go off to meditate, contemplate, and try to answer this seemingly impossible enigma.

One time, though, a Zen Monk presented this koan to a young child. "Remember," said the monk, "there are only two rules; you cannot kill the goose, and you cannot break the bottle. How do you get the goose out?"

The child thought about it for a moment and responded, "You break the bottle."

The point is that even if someone tells you (or you tell yourself) that there are certain rules that you must follow in order to become who you want to become or create what you want to create, the truth is that you always have the choice to be a Self-Leader in your experience. Thus, you choose what rules will set up the conditions to help you reach your desired outcome; what rules will stack the deck in your favor and set you up to win.

Honor yourself, create your rules, be empowered by them, and free your goose in whatever way you choose!

Small Ideas
Can Change Your Life

A single idea from the human mind can build cities. An idea can transform the world and rewrite all the rules.

—Leonardo DiCaprio as Dominic Cobb, *Inception*

What I would add to that insightful quote is that it is often the simplicity of those ideas that can have a huge transformational effect on our lives. Of course, it is sexy to create a car like the Tesla or a tablet like the iPad, with all of their bells, whistles, and technological advances. But the far less sexy inventions, the ones that don't require years of research, billions of dollars of investment, or global development teams, also have the potential to make a deep and profound impact on our lives. I see this in my coaching all the time.

A client who swaps out a single word and starts pursuing *excellence* instead of being a Prisoner to the quest for *perfection*, instantly feels lighter and more inspired to take action when they were otherwise anxious or feeling stuck.

With a simple reframe, someone I am working with who has lost their job can see this loss as a gift that will allow them to refocus their energy and attention on the thing their heart has been calling them to do. It shifts them from feeling burdensome and desperate to a fun and creative place to approach their next opportunity.

Interestingly enough, it isn't the word or the reframe that makes the biggest difference. It is the people who choose to own this new language or perspective, and the possibilities they create as a result, who ultimately create a new reality for themselves. "For themselves" is key, because Self-Leadership cannot be taught, imparted, bestowed, or granted from the outside in. Instead, it originates, grows, and becomes a part of one's being from the inside out. All it takes is a bit of awareness and a willingness to experiment with a new way of seeing how the world and the mind truly work.

Here is an absurd example that I hope will drive the point home in spite of its nonsensical nature. Imagine that for your entire life up to this moment, you did nothing but inhale when breathing. It was such an uncomfortable way to breathe, and it always felt like something was missing, but it was just the way you did it. Perhaps you were taught only to inhale by a close friend or family member. Or maybe you had some judgment about people who tried doing something more than just inhaling, so to make sure you didn't become those people, you stuck to your intake of air only.

Now picture that I saw you in line at the grocery store, and you were doing this shallow, "half-lunged" (I figured that was more

appropriate that half-a**ed) respiration, so I sat you down and introduced you to…exhaling.

Instantly, your world could be changed. That one simple shift, which would take me five seconds to explain and demonstrate, would give you 100% more options for how you could breathe than you knew existed just five seconds earlier. Not because I'm smarter or better or more enlightened than you, but because someone most certainly did the same for me at one point when I was committed to only breathing in.

Of course, it would then be up to you whether you test it out for yourself after we part ways—that is your moment-by-moment choice as a Self-Leader.

You could choose to be resistant because it isn't the way you have done it in the past or because you are worried about what people may think of you for doing such a bold thing. But the awareness is now there. And once you see it, and you understand it, you can't un-understand it.

So by all means, use your creativity, your words, and your ideas to end global hunger, eradicate deadly diseases, and create the next great era of technology. But please do not underestimate the power you have as a Self-Leader in your own life, and the impact you can have in the lives of others as a result, by paying attention to simple ideas that have the potential for transformation—if you slow down enough to see and test them for yourself.

This book is full of them. Which ones will you test out for yourself?

Tear Out This Page and Keep It with You

But don't read it until you've read the rest of this book. Reading this part too early may be too much to bear.

It makes freedom, peace, prosperity, and happiness deceptively simple and could cause you to throw the whole book away.

But once you are ready, once you understand how a Prison Break and shift to Self-Leadership truly occur, slow down and read this. Meditate on it anytime you need a reminder of the simplicity of shifting from a Prisoner to a Self-Leader instantly.

Being a Self-Leader is a choice

Being a Prisoner is a choice

Love is a choice

Fear is a choice

Slowing down is a choice

Self-acceptance is a choice

Playfulness is a choice

Resistance is a choice

Commitment is a choice

Your language is a choice

Your interpretations are a choice

Your response is a choice

Your possibilities are a choice

Your prosperity is a choice

Courage is a choice

Stress is a choice

Creating stories is a choice

Believing stories is a choice

Getting started is a choice

Continuing is a choice

Creativity is a choice

Overwhelm is a choice

Thinking this is complete nonsense is a choice

Choosing to live this way, just for today, is a choice.

"No matter what problem you may have to face today, there is a solution, because you have nothing to deal with but your own thoughts. As you know, you have the power to select and control your thoughts, difficult though it may be at times to do so. As long as you think that your destiny is in the hands of other people, the situation is hopeless. ...[Y]ou have nothing to deal with but your own thoughts.

Remind yourself of this fact constantly. ... Write it down where you will see it often. Have it on your desk... Hang it in your bedroom... Write it in your pocketbook. Write it on your soul... It will transform your life."

—Emmet Fox

References

Binazir, A. (2011, June 16). Are You a Miracle? On the Probability of Your Being Born [Web log post]. Retrieved June 7, 2016, from http://www.huffingtonpost.com/dr-ali-binazir/probability-being-born_b_877853.html

Demetri Martin Quotes. (n.d.). Retrieved June 7, 2016, from http://www.brainyquote.com/quotes/quotes/d/demetrimar416825.html

Fox, E. (2013). *Find and Use Your Inner Power*. Retrieved from http://books.google.com

Gorkin, C. (n.d.). "Worst Day Ever?" Retrieved May 12, 2016, from http://www.poetrynation.com/poem.php?id=50509

Vendera, J. (2008). *Raise Your Voice*. Retrieved from http://books.google.com

About the Author

What does an award-winning entrepreneur, a TEDx speaker, a baconatarian (that's a vegetarian who still eats bacon), a former rapper (who opened for the Wu-Tang Clan —YES, really!), and previously 332-pound man (who has since lost over 130 pounds despite his affinity for bacon) have in common?

They are all the same guy!

Jason "JG" Goldberg is an international "edu-tainer" and speaker, author of the #1 International Best-Seller **"Prison Break"** and creator of both the **Playful Prosperity** AND the **Competition-Proof Business Academy** programs.

He has been a featured expert or guest on traditional media outlets including ABC, CBS, and FOX as well as teaching on the Mindvalley and SoulPancake platforms and creating a business in partnership with NASA and the space shuIIe program while earning his MBA in graduate school!

Now JG focuses on blending his signature mix of simple and transformational wisdom, practical business mentorship, and belly-busting humor to help coaches, speakers and online educators build "Competition-PROOF" businesses full of impact and influence (and have a ton of FUN in the process)!

As a sought-after international speaker and host, JG has shared the stage with some of the world's greatest thought-leaders and innovators in human potential and performance including Jason Silva (Host of Nat Geo's "Brain Games"), Dr. Sean Stephenson (The 3 Foot Giant), Don Miguel Ruiz (The Four Agreements), Vishen Lakhiani (CEO of Mindvalley), Steven Kotler (Stealing Fire), Marisa Peer (the UK's psychotherapist to the stars) and so many others that he hopes will impress you if these other ones don't! ;)

To learn more about JG's Playful Prosperity program, head over to www.PlayfulProsperity.com.

And if you are a coach, speaker or online educator, you can get a free copy of JG's latest book **"How To Build a Competition-Proof Coaching Business"** here: http://BeCompetitionProof.com.

Made in the USA
Columbia, SC
27 September 2019